The Enforcement of Morals

The
Enforcement
of Morals

Patrick Devlin

amagi
an imprint of Liberty Fund, Inc.

Liberty Fund

Amagi books are published by Liberty Fund, Inc.
a foundation established to encourage study of the
ideal of a society of free and responsible individuals.

𒀀𒈣𒄀

The cuneiform inscription that serves as our logo and as a
design element for Liberty Fund books is the earliest-known
written appearance of the word "freedom" (*amagi*), or "liberty."
It is taken from a clay document written about 2300 B.C.
in the Sumerian city-state of Lagash.

This 2009 Liberty Fund edition is reproduced from the edition
published by Oxford University Press, Inc., 1970.

5th printing (2023)

Library of Congress Cataloging-in-Publication Data

Devlin, Patrick, Baron, 1905–1992.
The enforcement of morals / Patrick Devlin.
    p. cm.
This 2009 Liberty Fund edition is reproduced from the edition
published by Oxford University Press, Inc., 1970.
Includes bibliographical references.
ISBN 978-0-86597-805-8 (pb)
1. Law and ethics. I. Title.
KF450.P8 D48 2009
340'.112–dc22   2009044573

Cover design by Richard Hendel, Chapel Hill, North Carolina

LIBERTY FUND, INC.
11301 North Meridian Street
Carmel, Indiana 46032
libertyfund.org

Preface

In 1958 I was invited to deliver the second Maccabaean Lecture in Jurisprudence of the British Academy, the first having been delivered by Lord Evershed, then Master of the Rolls. It was an honour not to be declined but yet to be accepted only with much misgiving. A man who has passed his life in the practice of the law is not as a rule well equipped to discourse on questions of jurisprudence and I was certainly no exception to that rule. Fortunately, as it seemed to me, there was a subject which was both topical and within my powers to handle. In September 1957 the Wolfenden Committee had made its report recommending that homosexual practices in private between consenting adults should no longer be a crime. I had read with complete approval its formulation of the functions of the criminal law in matters of morality.

I had in fact given evidence before the Committee. Lord Goddard, then Lord Chief Justice, thought it desirable that evidence should be given by one judge of the Queen's Bench who thought that the law should not be altered and by another who was in favour of reform. I was in favour of reform. I agree with everyone who has written or spoken on the subject that homosexuality is usually a miserable way of life and that it is the duty of society, if it can, to save any youth from being led into it. I think that that duty has to be discharged although it may mean much suffering by incurable perverts who seem unable to resist the corruption of boys. But if there is no danger of corruption, I do not think that there is any good the law can do that outweighs the misery that exposure and imprisonment causes to addicts who cannot find satisfaction in any other way of life. Punishment will not cure and because it is haphazard in its incidence I doubt if it deters. Those who are detected and prosecuted are unlucky; and the full offence is frequently proved only because one or the other in his weakness confesses. I do not think that any judge now imposes a severe sentence in such cases. I cannot myself recollect ever having passed a sentence of imprisonment at all.

There is to my mind only one really powerful argument against reform and I put it in the form of a question. Can homosexuals be divided into those who corrupt youth and those who do not? If they cannot, is there a danger that the abolition of the offence between consenting adults might lead to an increase in corruption? The Wolfenden Committee thought that there was a division of this sort.[1] Some judges of great experience for whose views I have a deep respect think otherwise. There is room for a more comprehensive study of case histories on this point than has, so far as I know, yet been made.

At any rate what I proposed to the Committee was one of those illogical compromises that would be rejected out of hand in any system of law that was not English. I suggested that, while the full offence of buggery should be retained, the lesser offences of indecent assault and gross indecency should be abolished unless the acts were committed on youths. It seemed to me that this compromise might go some way towards meeting the fears of those who thought that the repeal of the Act would be an admission that buggery should be tolerated. It would afford time to see whether offences against youths increased and, if it were found to be so, the way back would be less difficult than if the Act had been totally repealed. It would result, I thought, in prosecutions for buggery being brought only in clear and flagrant cases, since the alternative of a conviction for the lesser offence would no longer be available. Anyway, it seemed to me as much as public opinion would be at all likely to support. The proposal was not favoured by the Committee and I dare say they were quite right.

All this of course has nothing to do with jurisprudence, and the only part of the Report relevant to that was the statement which, as I have said, I completely approved, that there was a realm of private morality which was not the law's business, and the distinction between crime and sin. I had never before thought about this distinction otherwise than superficially. I was aware that it derived its force from the teachings of Bentham and Mill. What I knew about their work was not very much and acquired at second-hand about a quarter of a century before. I had never read Mill's *On Liberty* from beginning to end and certainly could not have put my finger on his celebrated definition of the function of the criminal law. But Mill's ideas, even when absorbed at second-hand, are so clear and definitive that they are likely to make a permanent impression on the least attentive student. That was their effect on me.

As to the subject-matter of my lecture, what I had in mind to do

---

[1] Wolfenden, paras. 56 and 57.

was to take other examples of private immorality and to show how they were affected by the criminal law and to consider what amendments would be necessary to make the law conform with the statement of principle in the Report. But study destroyed instead of confirming the simple faith in which I had begun my task; and the Maccabaean Lecture, the first in this book, is a statement of the reasons which persuaded me that I was wrong.

I did not then know that the same ground had already been covered by Mr. Justice Stephen in his book *Liberty, Equality, Fraternity* published in 1873. It was not until much later that I was with great difficulty able to obtain from the Holborn Public Library a copy of the book held together with an elastic band. I hope that, as a result of Professor Hart's criticism of it, more interest will now be aroused in a valuable work. Although I missed altogether one cogent argument advanced by Stephen, I find great similarity between his view and mine on the principles which should affect the use of the criminal law for the enforcement of morals.[1] Commenting on the work of Mr. Justice Stephen and myself, P. ofessor Hart noted that 'the similarity in the general tone and sometimes in the detail of their argument is very great'.[2] The fact that we reached our conclusions independently gives additional force to Professor Hart's comment (which, however it may have been intended, I regard as complimentary) that they reveal 'the outlook characteristic of the English judiciary'.[3]

The Maccabaean Lecture aroused an interest greater than it deserved. There is a number of reasons for this. It was delivered by a judge and judges in their rare extra-judicial utterances usually confine themselves to the working of the law. I have explained how it was that I was driven into deeper waters. It was almost immediately denounced in rather strong language by the distinguished jurist Professor Hart in a piece which has been given a place among the masterpieces of English legal prose in *The Law as Literature*. It was an expression of orthodox views on a subject in which orthodoxy is more seldom found in print than it is in common behaviour. Although not itself concerned with any particular morality, it came at a time when the conflict between old and new moralities was being given a sharper edge.

[1] Stephen, at p. 172, sets out four 'great leading principles'.
[2] H. L. A. Hart, *Law, Liberty and Morality*, Oxford University Press, 1963, p. 16.
[3] ibid. p. 63.

Consequently it has since been referred to in a number of articles and I have listed at page xiii all of them known to me. I have of course paid great attention to the criticisms they contain. I do not want to alter anything that I wrote but I think that at one point the emphasis might be reduced. That is the emphasis on the part which 'feeling' plays in the judgement of the reasonable man. I put the word in quotation marks because I am not sure that I use it in its correct philosophical sense. I find that I used the words 'right' and 'ought' in a sense which would be likely to be understood by most readers of the law reports, but not by philosophers.[1] What I want is a word that would clarify the distinction between 'rational' and 'reasonable'. The reasonable man is to be expected not to hold an irrational belief. The Emperor Justinian, Professor Hart says, stated that homosexuality was the cause of earthquakes.[2] That may have been a rational belief in the Emperor's time, but now that we know a good deal more about earthquakes and a little more about homosexuality, we can safely say that it would be irrational so to believe. But when the irrational is excluded, there is, as any judge and juryman knows, a number of conclusions left for all of which some good reasons can be urged. The exclusion of the irrational is usually an easy and comparatively unimportant process. For the difficult choice between a number of rational conclusions the ordinary man has to rely upon a 'feeling' for the right answer. Reasoning will get him nowhere.

It may be that the language I used put too much emphasis on feeling and too little on reason. Even so, I think that the intense criticism which has been focused on the words 'intolerance, indignation and disgust' (which I do not wish to modify) was on any view excessive. To assert or to imply—both assertion and implication have been very frequently employed—that the author would like to see the criminal law used to stamp out whatever makes the ordinary man sick hardly does justice to the argument.

The phrase is not used in that part of the argument which discusses how the common morality should be ascertained but in that part of it which enumerates the factors which should restrict the use of the criminal law. It comes into the discussion of the first factor which is that there must be toleration of the maximum individual freedom that is consistent with the integrity of society.

---

[1] See, for example, the article by Professor Wollheim, listed in the bibliography, p. xiv.   [2] Hart, *Law, Liberty and Morality*, p. 50.

It must be read in subjection to the statement that the judgement which the community passes on a practice which it dislikes must be calm and dispassionate and that mere disapproval is not enough to justify interference. There may be some who think that intolerance and disgust can never be the product of calm and dispassionate consideration and if so I would disagree. I do not know any sensible person who does not occasionally get indignant and disgusted about something, even if it is only at the idea of somebody else's disgust about something that does not disgust him. If there is not that intensity of feeling, so my argument runs, the collective judgement should not be given the force of law. There are to be found in any community individuals, always the most vocal, who are easily swayed and perhaps irrationally moved to indignation and disgust. But my experience of the average Englishman, which may differ from that of my critics, but which is founded on long observation of the juryman who personifies the average Englishman operating in surroundings which induce to calmness and dispassion, is that he is not easily moved to indignation and disgust. At least there can be no doubt that the number of those who strongly disapprove of a practice such as homosexuality would be far greater than the number of those who view it with disgust or indignation; and that is the point of the paragraph.

The other lectures all stem from the Maccabaean Lecture and discuss different aspects of the relationship between law and morals that are suggested by it. The Maccabaean Lecture discussed the relationship between the moral law and the criminal law but was confined to those sorts of crime that can also be called sins. The second, third, and fourth lectures consider the moral law in relation to other branches of English law—the quasi-criminal law, the law of tort, the laws of contract and of marriage. Some of the points made in the second lecture have been blunted by subsequent judicial activity in which I have participated. The fifth lecture discusses the difficult question of how to determine for the purposes of the secular law what the moral law is. The sixth examines once again Mill's teaching, which, although as a whole it has never been adopted, is still the mainspring of liberal thought on this subject. The seventh, which is perhaps of interest only to controversialists, inquires what sort of doctrine, if any, is likely to replace Mill's.

The two themes in the lectures that have attracted most criticism are, firstly, the denial that there is a private realm of morality into which the law cannot enter; and secondly, the assertion that the morality which the law enforces must be popular morality. So far the criticism has been destructive in character, offering an opening for some further positive thought on both these points.

The criticism of the denial that there is a private realm has been conducted in accordance with the principle that attack is the best form of defence. It has not thrown any light upon what exactly the realm is and what it contains. The doctrine is known to be derived from Mill but few of its supporters accept the whole of Mill's teaching. I should like to see someone better equipped than myself take up the task which I began, before (as the critics would have it) I fell into error; and explain how far the doctrine goes and what its impact would be on the existing criminal law. There is need for some heavy constructive work here. As I suggest in the last lecture in this book, what is likely to emerge is a radical restatement.

On the second point I should not care, any more than my critics would, to have my personal morality equated with that which gains the highest measure of popular approval. But the question is not how a person is to ascertain the morality which he adopts and follows, but how the law is to ascertain the morality which it enforces. The question is not evaded by saying that the law ought not to enforce any morality at all because everyone is agreed that it ought to protect the morals of youth. It is not answered by saying that the law ought to enforce the morality taught by some religion unless adherence to that religious belief is made compulsory. Nor is it answered by substituting reason for revelation unless it can be asserted that there is only one sort of morality that can be arrived at rationally. I attempt an answer in the fifth lecture in this book. It is now the turn of those who find the answer unacceptable to say what the right answer is.

Indeed, the best justification for printing this collection of lectures is the possibility that it may stimulate the professionals to undertake not merely the demolition of amateur work but the construction of something better.

Only the first and second lectures have previously appeared in print in Britain. The fifth and sixth have appeared in print in the United States. I must acknowledge in each case the courtesy of those bodies under whose auspices the lectures were given and my gratitude to those who have given permission to reprint where that was necessary.

Contents

Bibliography

Friedmann, Professor W., in the *Natural Law Forum*, Notre Dame, Indiana, 1964, vol. 4, p. 151.

Hart, Professor H. L. A. 'Immorality and Treason', *The Listener*, 30 July 1959, p. 162. Reprinted in *The Law as Literature*, edited by L. J. Blom-Cooper, Bodley Head, 1961.
  Law, Liberty and Morality, Oxford University Press, 1963. Cited as 'Hart'.

Henkin, Professor Louis. 'Morals and the Constitution: the Sin of Obscenity', *Columbia Law Review*, 1963, vol. 63, p. 393.

Hughes, Graham. 'Morals and the Criminal Law', *Yale Law Journal*, 1961, vol. 71, p. 622.

Hurt, Robert M. 'Sin and the Criminal Law', *New Individualist Review*, 1962, vol. 2, p. 29.

Gilby, Thomas, O.P. 'The Crimination of Sin', *Blackfriars*, 1960, vol. 41, p. 53.

Ginsberg, Morris. 'Law and Morals', *The British Journal of Criminology*, January 1964, p. 283.

Mewett, Alan W. 'Morality and the Criminal Law', *University of Toronto Law Journal*, 1962, vol. 14, p. 213.

Mill, John Stuart. *On Liberty*, London, 1859. Reprinted in *Utilitarianism, Liberty and Representative Government*, 1910, Everyman's Library, no. 482. Cited as 'Mill'.[1]

Moore, E. Garth. 'A Moral Approach to Law', *Crucible*, January 1964, p. 29.

Rostow, Eugene. 'The Enforcement of Morals', *Cambridge Law Journal*, November 1960, p. 174. Reprinted in *The Sovereign Prerogative*, Yale University Press, 1962.

[1] So that the citations may more easily be identified in other editions, I give below the chapter numbers and paging in the Everyman edition.

Chapter I p. 65
II 78
III 114
IV 131
V 149

St. John-Stevas, Norman. *Life, Death and the Law*. Eyre and Spottiswoode, 1961.

Stephen, James FitzJames, Q.C. *Liberty, Equality, Fraternity*, 2nd ed., Smith Elgard & Co., London, 1874. Cited as 'Stephen'.

Summers, Professor Robert S., in *New York University Law Review*, vol. 38, p. 1201.

'Wolfenden Report'. Report of the Committee on Homosexual Offences and Prostitution, 1957, Cmd. 247. Cited as 'Wolfenden'.

Wollheim, Richard. 'Crime, Sin and Mr. Justice Devlin', *Encounter*, November 1959, p. 34.

Wootton, Barbara. *Crime and the Criminal Law*, Stevens & Sons, London, 1963, pp. 41 ff.

I

Morals and the Criminal Law*

The Report of the Committee on Homosexual Offences and Prostitution, generally known as the Wolfenden Report, is recognized to be an excellent study of two very difficult legal and social problems. But it has also a particular claim to the respect of those interested in jurisprudence; it does what law reformers so rarely do; it sets out clearly and carefully what in relation to its subjects it considers the function of the law to be.[1] Statutory additions to the criminal law are too often made on the simple principle that 'there ought to be a law against it'. The greater part of the law relating to sexual offences is the creation of statute and it is difficult to ascertain any logical relationship between it and the moral ideas which most of us uphold. Adultery, fornication, and prostitution are not, as the Report[2] points out, criminal offences: homosexuality between males is a criminal offence, but between females it is not. Incest was not an offence until it was declared so by statute only fifty years ago. Does the legislature select these offences haphazardly or are there some principles which can be used to determine what part of the moral law should be embodied in the criminal? There is, for example, being now considered a proposal to make A.I.D., that is, the practice of artificial insemination of a woman with the seed of a man who is not her husband, a criminal offence; if, as is usually the case, the woman is married, this is in substance, if not in form, adultery. Ought it to be made punishable when adultery is not? This sort of

---

* Maccabaean Lecture in Jurisprudence read at the British Academy on 18 March 1959 and printed in the *Proceedings of the British Academy*, vol. xlv, under the title 'The Enforcement of Morals'.

[1] The Committee's 'statement of juristic philosophy' (to quote Lord Pakenham) was considered by him in a debate in the House of Lords on 4 December 1957, reported in *Hansard Lords Debates*, vol. ccvi at 738; and also in the same debate by the Archbishop of Canterbury at 753 and Lord Denning at 806. The subject has also been considered by Mr. J. E. Hall Williams in the *Law Quarterly Review*, January 1958, vol. lxxiv, p. 76.

[2] Para. 14.

question is of practical importance, for a law that appears to be arbitrary and illogical, in the end and after the wave of moral indignation that has put it on the statute book subsides, forfeits respect. As a practical question it arises more frequently in the field of sexual morals than in any other, but there is no special answer to be found in that field. The inquiry must be general and fundamental. What is the connexion between crime and sin and to what extent, if at all, should the criminal law of England concern itself with the enforcement of morals and punish sin or immorality as such?

The statements of principle in the Wolfenden Report provide an admirable and modern starting-point for such an inquiry. In the course of my examination of them I shall find matter for criticism. If my criticisms are sound, it must not be imagined that they point to any shortcomings in the Report. Its authors were not, as I am trying to do, composing a paper on the jurisprudence of morality; they were evolving a working formula to use for reaching a number of practical conclusions. I do not intend to express any opinion one way or the other about these; that would be outside the scope of a lecture on jurisprudence. I am concerned only with general principles; the statement of these in the Report illuminates the entry into the subject and I hope that its authors will forgive me if I carry the lamp with me into places where it was not intended to go.

Early in the Report[1] the Committee put forward:

Our own formulation of the function of the criminal law so far as it concerns the subjects of this enquiry. In this field, its function, as we see it, is to preserve public order and decency, to protect the citizen from what is offensive or injurious, and to provide sufficient safeguards against exploitation and corruption of others, particularly those who are specially vulnerable because they are young, weak in body or mind, inexperienced, or in a state of special physical, official or economic dependence.

It is not, in our view, the function of the law to intervene in the private lives of citizens, or to seek to enforce any particular pattern of behaviour, further than is necessary to carry out the purposes we have outlined.

The Committee preface their most important recommendation[2]

that homosexual behaviour between consenting adults in private should no longer be a criminal offence, [by stating the argument[3]] which we believe to be decisive, namely, the importance which society and the law ought to give to individual freedom of choice and action in matters of

---

[1] Para. 13.   [2] Para. 62.   [3] Para. 61.

private morality. Unless a deliberate attempt is to be made by society, acting through the agency of the law, to equate the sphere of crime with that of sin, there must remain a realm of private morality and immorality which is, in brief and crude terms, not the law's business. To say this is not to condone or encourage private immorality.

Similar statements of principle are set out in the chapters of the Report which deal with prostitution. No case can be sustained, the Report says, for attempting to make prostitution itself illegal.[1] The Committee refer to the general reasons already given and add: 'We are agreed that private immorality should not be the concern of the criminal law except in the special circumstances therein mentioned.' They quote[2] with approval the report of the Street Offences Committee,[3] which says: 'As a general proposition it will be universally accepted that the law is not concerned with private morals or with ethical sanctions.' It will be observed that the emphasis is on *private* immorality. By this is meant immorality which is not offensive or injurious to the public in the ways defined or described in the first passage which I quoted. In other words, no act of immorality should be made a criminal offence unless it is accompanied by some other feature such as indecency, corruption, or exploitation. This is clearly brought out in relation to prostitution: 'It is not the duty of the law to concern itself with immorality as such . . . it should confine itself to those activities which offend against public order and decency or expose the ordinary citizen to what is offensive or injurious.'[4]

These statements of principle are naturally restricted to the subject-matter of the Report. But they are made in general terms and there seems to be no reason why, if they are valid, they should not be applied to the criminal law in general. They separate very decisively crime from sin, the divine law from the secular, and the moral from the criminal. They do not signify any lack of support for the law, moral or criminal, and they do not represent an attitude that can be called either religious or irreligious. There are many schools of thought among those who may think that morals are not the law's business. There is first of all the agnostic or free-thinker. He does not of course disbelieve in morals, nor in sin if it be given the wider of the two meanings assigned to it in the *Oxford English Dictionary* where it is defined as 'transgression against divine law or the principles of morality'. He cannot accept the divine law; that does not

---

[1] Para. 224.　　　[2] Para. 227.　　　[3] Cmd. 3231 (1928).　　　[4] Para. 257.

mean that he might not view with suspicion any departure from moral principles that have for generations been accepted by the society in which he lives; but in the end he judges for himself. Then there is the deeply religious person who feels that the criminal law is sometimes more of a hindrance than a help in the sphere of morality, and that the reform of the sinner—at any rate when he injures only himself—should be a spiritual rather than a temporal work. Then there is the man who without any strong feeling cannot see why, where there is freedom in religious belief, there should not logically be freedom in morality as well. All these are powerfully allied against the equating of crime with sin.

I must disclose at the outset that I have as a judge an interest in the result of the inquiry which I am seeking to make as a juris-prudent. As a judge who administers the criminal law and who has often to pass sentence in a criminal court, I should feel handicapped in my task if I thought that I was addressing an audience which had no sense of sin or which thought of crime as something quite differ-ent. Ought one, for example, in passing sentence upon a female abortionist to treat her simply as if she were an unlicensed midwife? If not, why not? But if so, is all the panoply of the law erected over a set of social regulations? I must admit that I begin with a feeling that a complete separation of crime from sin (I use the term through-out this lecture in the wider meaning) would not be good for the moral law and might be disastrous for the criminal. But can this sort of feeling be justified as a matter of jurisprudence? And if it be a right feeling, how should the relationship between the criminal and the moral law be stated? Is there a good theoretical basis for it, or is it just a practical working alliance, or is it a bit of both? That is the problem which I want to examine, and I shall begin by considering the standpoint of the strict logician. It can be supported by cogent arguments, some of which I believe to be unanswerable and which I put as follows.

Morals and religion are inextricably joined—the moral standards generally accepted in Western civilization being those belonging to Christianity. Outside Christendom other standards derive from other religions. None of these moral codes can claim any validity except by virtue of the religion on which it is based. Old Testament morals differ in some respects from New Testament morals. Even within Christianity there are differences. Some hold that contracep-tion is an immoral practice and that a man who has carnal knowledge of another woman while his wife is alive is in all circumstances a fornicator; others, including most of the English-speaking world, deny both these propositions. Between the great religions of the world, of which Christianity is only one, there are much wider differences. It may or may not be right for the State to adopt one of these religions as the truth, to found itself upon its doctrines, and to deny to any of its citizens the liberty to practise any other. If it does, it is logical that it should use the secular law wherever it thinks it necessary to enforce the divine. If it does not, it is illogical that it should concern itself with morals as such. But if it leaves matters of religion to private judgement, it should logically leave matters of morals also. A State which refuses to enforce Christian beliefs has lost the right to enforce Christian morals.

If this view is sound, it means that the criminal law cannot justify any of its provisions by reference to the moral law. It cannot say, for example, that murder and theft are prohibited because they are immoral or sinful. The State must justify in some other way the punishments which it imposes on wrongdoers and a function for the criminal law independent of morals must be found. This is not difficult to do. The smooth functioning of society and the preservation of order require that a number of activities should be regulated. The rules that are made for that purpose and are enforced by the criminal law are often designed simply to achieve uniformity and convenience and rarely involve any choice between good and evil. Rules that impose a speed limit or prevent obstruction on the highway have nothing to do with morals. Since so much of the criminal law is composed of rules of this sort, why bring morals into it at all? Why not define the function of the criminal law in simple terms as the preservation of order and decency and the protection of the lives and property of citizens, and elaborate those terms in relation to any particular subject in the way in which it is done in the Wolfenden Report? The criminal law in carrying out these objects will undoubtedly overlap the moral law. Crimes of violence are morally wrong and they are also offences against good order; therefore they offend against both laws. But this is simply because the two laws in pursuit of different objectives happen to cover the same area. Such is the argument.

Is the argument consistent or inconsistent with the fundamental principles of English criminal law as it exists today? That is the first way of testing it, though by no means a conclusive one. In the field of jurisprudence one is at liberty to overturn even fundamental conceptions if they are theoretically unsound. But to see how the argument fares under the existing law is a good starting-point.

It is true that for many centuries the criminal law was much concerned with keeping the peace and little, if at all, with sexual morals. But it would be wrong to infer from that that it had no moral content or that it would ever have tolerated the idea of a man being left to judge for himself in matters of morals. The criminal law of England has from the very first concerned itself with moral principles. A simple way of testing this point is to consider the attitude which the criminal law adopts towards consent.

Subject to certain exceptions inherent in the nature of particular crimes, the criminal law has never permitted consent of the victim to be used as a defence. In rape, for example, consent negatives an essential element. But consent of the victim is no defence to a charge of murder. It is not a defence to any form of assault that the victim thought his punishment well deserved and submitted to it; to make a good defence the accused must prove that the law gave him the right to chastise and that he exercised it reasonably. Likewise, the victim may not forgive the aggressor and require the prosecution to desist; the right to enter a *nolle prosequi* belongs to the Attorney-General alone.

Now, if the law existed for the protection of the individual, there would be no reason why he should avail himself of it if he did not want it. The reason why a man may not consent to the commission of an offence against himself beforehand or forgive it afterwards is because it is an offence against society. It is not that society is physically injured; that would be impossible. Nor need any individual be shocked, corrupted, or exploited; everything may be done in private. Nor can it be explained on the practical ground that a violent man is a potential danger to others in the community who have therefore a direct interest in his apprehension and punishment as being necessary to their own protection. That would be true of a man whom the victim is prepared to forgive but not of one who gets his consent first; a murderer who acts only upon the consent, and maybe the request, of his victim is no menace to others, but he does threaten one of the great moral principles upon which society is based, that is, the sanctity of human life. There is only one explanation of what has hitherto been accepted as the basis of the criminal law and that is that there are certain standards of behaviour or moral principles which society requires to be observed; and the breach of them is an offence not merely against the person who is injured but against society as a whole.

Thus, if the criminal law were to be reformed so as to eliminate from it everything that was not designed to preserve order and decency or to protect citizens (including the protection of youth from corruption), it would overturn a fundamental principle. It would also end a number of specific crimes. Euthanasia or the killing of another at his own request, suicide, attempted suicide and suicide pacts, duelling, abortion, incest between brother and sister, are all acts which can be done in private and without offence to others and need not involve the corruption or exploitation of others. Many people think that the law on some of these subjects is in need of reform, but no one hitherto has gone so far as to suggest that they should all be left outside the criminal law as matters of private morality. They can be brought within it only as a matter of moral principle. It must be remembered also that although there is much immorality that is not punished by the law, there is none that is condoned by the law. The law will not allow its processes to be used by those engaged in immorality of any sort. For example, a house may not be let for immoral purposes; the lease is invalid and would not be enforced. But if what goes on inside there is a matter of private morality and not the law's business, why does the law inquire into it at all?

I think it is clear that the criminal law as we know it is based upon moral principle. In a number of crimes its function is simply to enforce a moral principle and nothing else. The law, both criminal and civil, claims to be able to speak about morality and immorality generally. Where does it get its authority to do this and how does it settle the moral principles which it enforces? Undoubtedly, as a matter of history, it derived both from Christian teaching. But I think that the strict logician is right when he says that the law can no longer rely on doctrines in which citizens are entitled to disbelieve. It is necessary therefore to look for some other source.

In jurisprudence, as I have said, everything is thrown open to discussion and, in the belief that they cover the whole field, I have framed three interrogatories addressed to myself to answer:

1. Has society the right to pass judgement at all on matters of morals? Ought there, in other words, to be a public morality, or are morals always a matter for private judgement?

2. If society has the right to pass judgement, has it also the right to use the weapon of the law to enforce it?

3. If so, ought it to use that weapon in all cases or only in some; and if only in some, on what principles should it distinguish?

I shall begin with the first interrogatory and consider what is meant by the right of society to pass a moral judgement, that is, a judgement about what is good and what is evil. The fact that a majority of people may disapprove of a practice does not of itself make it a matter for society as a whole. Nine men out of ten may disapprove of what the tenth man is doing and still say that it is not their business. There is a case for a collective judgement (as distinct from a large number of individual opinions which sensible people may even refrain from pronouncing at all if it is upon somebody else's private affairs) only if society is affected. Without a collective judgement there can be no case at all for intervention. Let me take as an illustration the Englishman's attitude to religion as it is now and as it has been in the past. His attitude now is that a man's religion is his private affair; he may think of another man's religion that it is right or wrong, true or untrue, but not that it is good or bad. In earlier times that was not so; a man was denied the right to practise what was thought of as heresy, and heresy was thought of as destructive of society.

The language used in the passages I have quoted from the Wolfenden Report suggests the view that there ought not to be a collective judgement about immorality *per se*. Is this what is meant by 'private morality' and 'individual freedom of choice and action'? Some people sincerely believe that homosexuality is neither immoral nor unnatural. Is the 'freedom of choice and action' that is offered to the individual, freedom to decide for himself what is moral or immoral, society remaining neutral; or is it freedom to be immoral if he wants to be? The language of the Report may be open to question, but the conclusions at which the Committee arrive answer this question unambiguously. If society is not prepared to say that homosexuality is morally wrong, there would be no basis for a law protecting youth from 'corruption' or punishing a man for living on the 'immoral' earnings of a homosexual prostitute, as the Report recommends.[1] This attitude the Committee make even clearer when they come to deal with prostitution. In truth, the Report takes it for

[1] Para. 76.

granted that there is in existence a public morality which condemns homosexuality and prostitution. What the Report seems to mean by private morality might perhaps be better described as private behaviour in matters of morals.

This view—that there is such a thing as public morality—can also be justified by *a priori* argument. What makes a society of any sort is community of ideas, not only political ideas but also ideas about the way its members should behave and govern their lives; these latter ideas are its morals. Every society has a moral structure as well as a political one: or rather, since that might suggest two independent systems, I should say that the structure of every society is made up both of politics and morals. Take, for example, the institution of marriage. Whether a man should be allowed to take more than one wife is something about which every society has to make up its mind one way or the other. In England we believe in the Christian idea of marriage and therefore adopt monogamy as a moral principle. Consequently the Christian institution of marriage has become the basis of family life and so part of the structure of our society. It is there not because it is Christian. It has got there because it is Christian, but it remains there because it is built into the house in which we live and could not be removed without bringing it down. The great majority of those who live in this country accept it because it is the Christian idea of marriage and for them the only true one. But a non-Christian is bound by it, not because it is part of Christianity but because, rightly or wrongly, it has been adopted by the society in which he lives. It would be useless for him to stage a debate designed to prove that polygamy was theologically more correct and socially preferable; if he wants to live in the house, he must accept it as built in the way in which it is.

We see this more clearly if we think of ideas or institutions that are purely political. Society cannot tolerate rebellion; it will not allow argument about the rightness of the cause. Historians a century later may say that the rebels were right and the Government was wrong and a percipient and conscientious subject of the State may think so at the time. But it is not a matter which can be left to individual judgement.

The institution of marriage is a good example for my purpose because it bridges the division, if there is one, between politics and morals. Marriage is part of the structure of our society and it is also the basis of a moral code which condemns fornication and adultery.

The institution of marriage would be gravely threatened if individual judgements were permitted about the morality of adultery; on these points there must be a public morality. But public morality is not to be confined to those moral principles which support institutions such as marriage. People do not think of monogamy as something which has to be supported because our society has chosen to organize itself upon it; they think of it as something that is good in itself and offering a good way of life and that it is for that reason that our society has adopted it. I return to the statement that I have already made, that society means a community of ideas; without shared ideas on politics, morals, and ethics no society can exist. Each one of us has ideas about what is good and what is evil; they cannot be kept private from the society in which we live. If men and women try to create a society in which there is no fundamental agreement about good and evil they will fail; if, having based it on common agreement, the agreement goes, the society will disintegrate. For society is not something that is kept together physically; it is held by the invisible bonds of common thought. If the bonds were too far relaxed the members would drift apart. A common morality is part of the bondage. The bondage is part of the price of society; and mankind, which needs society, must pay its price.

Common lawyers used to say that Christianity was part of the law of the land. That was never more than a piece of rhetoric as Lord Sumner said in *Bowman* v. *The Secular Society*.[1] What lay behind it was the notion which I have been seeking to expound, namely that morals—and up till a century or so ago no one thought it worth distinguishing between religion and morals—were necessary to the temporal order. In 1675 Chief Justice Hale said: 'To say that religion is a cheat is to dissolve all those obligations whereby civil society is preserved.'[2] In 1797 Mr. Justice Ashurst said of blasphemy that it was 'not only an offence against God but against all law and government from its tendency to dissolve all the bonds and obligations of civil society'.[3] By 1908 Mr. Justice Phillimore was able to say: ' A man is free to think, to speak and to teach what he pleases as to religious matters, but not as to morals.'[4]

You may think that I have taken far too long in contending that there is such a thing as public morality, a proposition which most people would readily accept, and may have left myself too little time

[1] (1917), A.C. 406, at 457.
[2] *Taylor's Case*, 1 Vent. 293.
[3] *R.* v. *Williams*, 26 St. Tr. 653, at 715.
[4] *R.* v. *Boulter*, 72 J.P. 188.

to discuss the next question which to many minds may cause greater difficulty: to what extent should society use the law to enforce its moral judgements? But I believe that the answer to the first question determines the way in which the second should be approached and may indeed very nearly dictate the answer to the second question. If society has no right to make judgements on morals, the law must find some special justification for entering the field of morality: if homosexuality and prostitution are not in themselves wrong, then the onus is very clearly on the lawgiver who wants to frame a law against certain aspects of them to justify the exceptional treatment. But if society has the right to make a judgement and has it on the basis that a recognized morality is as necessary to society as, say, a recognized government, then society may use the law to preserve morality in the same way as it uses it to safeguard anything else that is essential to its existence. If therefore the first proposition is securely established with all its implications, society has a prima facie right to legislate against immorality as such.

The Wolfenden Report, notwithstanding that it seems to admit the right of society to condemn homosexuality and prostitution as immoral, requires special circumstances to be shown to justify the intervention of the law. I think that this is wrong in principle and that any attempt to approach my second interrogatory on these lines is bound to break down. I think that the attempt by the Committee does break down and that this is shown by the fact that it has to define or describe its special circumstances so widely that they can be supported only if it is accepted that the law *is* concerned with immorality as such.

The widest of the special circumstances are described as the provision of 'sufficient safeguards against exploitation and corruption of others, particularly those who are specially vulnerable because they are young, weak in body or mind, inexperienced, or in a state of special physical, official or economic dependence'.[1] The corruption of youth is a well-recognized ground for intervention by the State and for the purpose of any legislation the young can easily be defined. But if similar protection were to be extended to every other citizen, there would be no limit to the reach of the law. The 'corruption and exploitation of others' is so wide that it could be used to cover any sort of immorality which involves, as most do, the co-operation of another person. Even if the phrase is taken as limited

---

[1] Para. 13.

to the categories that are particularized as 'specially vulnerable', it is so elastic as to be practically no restriction. This is not merely a matter of words. For if the words used are stretched almost beyond breaking-point, they still are not wide enough to cover the recommendations which the Committee make about prostitution.

Prostitution is not in itself illegal and the Committee do not think that it ought to be made so.[1] If prostitution is private immorality and not the law's business, what concern has the law with the ponce or the brothel-keeper or the householder who permits habitual prostitution? The Report recommends that the laws which make these activities criminal offences should be maintained or strengthened and brings them (so far as it goes into principle; with regard to brothels it says simply that the law rightly frowns on them) under the head of exploitation.[2] There may be cases of exploitation in this trade, as there are or used to be in many others, but in general a ponce exploits a prostitute no more than an impresario exploits an actress. The Report finds that 'the great majority of prostitutes are women whose psychological makeup is such that they choose this life because they find in it a style of living which is to them easier, freer and more profitable than would be provided by any other occupation. . . . In the main the association between prostitute and ponce is voluntary and operates to mutual advantage.'[3] The Committee would agree that this could not be called exploitation in the ordinary sense. They say: 'It is in our view an over-simplification to think that those who live on the earnings of prostitution are exploiting the prostitute as such. What they are really exploiting is the whole complex of the relationship between prostitute and customer; they are, in effect, exploiting the human weaknesses which cause the customer to seek the prostitute and the prostitute to meet the demand.'[4]

All sexual immorality involves the exploitation of human weaknesses. The prostitute exploits the lust of her customers and the customer the moral weakness of the prostitute. If the exploitation of human weaknesses is considered to create a special circumstance, there is virtually no field of morality which can be defined in such a way as to exclude the law.

I think, therefore, that it is not possible to set theoretical limits to the power of the State to legislate against immorality. It is not

[1] Paras. 224, 285, and 318.   [2] Paras. 302 and 320.
[3] Para. 223.   [4] Para. 306.

possible to settle in advance exceptions to the general rule or to define inflexibly areas of morality into which the law is in no circumstances to be allowed to enter. Society is entitled by means of its laws to protect itself from dangers, whether from within or without. Here again I think that the political parallel is legitimate. The law of treason is directed against aiding the king's enemies and against sedition from within. The justification for this is that established government is necessary for the existence of society and therefore its safety against violent overthrow must be secured. But an established morality is as necessary as good government to the welfare of society. Societies disintegrate from within more frequently than they are broken up by external pressures. There is disintegration when no common morality is observed and history shows that the loosening of moral bonds is often the first stage of disintegration, so that society is justified in taking the same steps to preserve its moral code as it does to preserve its government and other essential institutions.[1] The suppression of vice is as much the law's business

[1] It is somewhere about this point in the argument that Professor Hart in *Law, Liberty and Morality* discerns a proposition which he describes as central to my thought. He states the proposition and his objection to it as follows (p. 51). 'He appears to move from the acceptable proposition that *some* shared morality is essential to the existence of any society [this I take to be the proposition on p. 12] to the unacceptable proposition that a society is identical with its morality as that is at any given moment of its history, so that a change in its morality is tantamount to the destruction of a society. The former proposition might be even accepted as a necessary rather than an empirical truth depending on a quite plausible definition of society as a body of men who hold certain moral views in common. But the latter proposition is absurd. Taken strictly, it would prevent us saying that the morality of a given society had changed, and would compel us instead to say that one society had disappeared and another one taken its place. But it is only on this absurd criterion of what it is for the same society to continue to exist that it could be asserted without evidence that any deviation from a society's shared morality threatens its existence.' In conclusion (p. 82) Professor Hart condemns the whole thesis in the lecture as based on 'a confused definition of what a society is'.

I do not assert that *any* deviation from a society's shared morality threatens its existence any more than I assert that *any* subversive activity threatens its existence. I assert that they are both activities which are capable in their nature of threatening the existence of society so that neither can be put beyond the law.

For the rest, the objection appears to me to be all a matter of words. I would venture to assert, for example, that you cannot have a game without rules and that if there were no rules there would be no game. If I am asked whether that means that the game is 'identical' with the rules, I would be willing for the question to be answered either way in the belief that the answer would lead to nowhere. If I am asked whether a change in the rules means that one game has disappeared and another has taken its place, I would reply probably not, but that it would depend on the extent of the change.

Likewise I should venture to assert that there cannot be a contract without terms. Does this mean that an 'amended' contract is a 'new' contract in the eyes of the law? I once listened to an argument by an ingenious counsel that a contract, because of the

as the suppression of subversive activities; it is no more possible to define a sphere of private morality than it is to define one of private subversive activity. It is wrong to talk of private morality or of the law not being concerned with immorality as such or to try to set rigid bounds to the part which the law may play in the suppression of vice. There are no theoretical limits to the power of the State to legislate against treason and sedition, and likewise I think there can be no theoretical limits to legislation against immorality. You may argue that if a man's sins affect only himself it cannot be the concern of society. If he chooses to get drunk every night in the privacy of his own home, is any one except himself the worse for it? But suppose a quarter or a half of the population got drunk every night, what sort of society would it be? You cannot set a theoretical limit to the number of people who can get drunk before society is entitled to legislate against drunkenness. The same may be said of gambling. The Royal Commission on Betting, Lotteries, and Gaming took as their test the character of the citizen as a member of society. They said: 'Our concern with the ethical significance of gambling is confined to the effect which it may have on the character of the gambler as a member of society. If we were convinced that whatever the degree of gambling this effect must be harmful we should be inclined to think that it was the duty of the state to restrict gambling to the greatest extent practicable.'[1]

In what circumstances the State should exercise its power is the third of the interrogatories I have framed. But before I get to it I must raise a point which might have been brought up in any one of the three. How are the moral judgements of society to be ascertained? By leaving it until now, I can ask it in the more limited form that is

substitution of one clause for another, had 'ceased to have effect' within the meaning of a statutory provision. The judge did not accept the argument; but if most of the fundamental terms had been changed, I daresay he would have done.

The proposition that I make in the text is that if (as I understand Professor Hart to agree, at any rate for the purposes of the argument) you cannot have a society without morality, the law can be used to enforce morality as something that is essential to a society. I cannot see why this proposition (whether it is right or wrong) should mean that morality can never be changed without the destruction of society. If morality is changed, the law can be changed. Professor Hart refers (p. 72) to the proposition as 'the use of legal punishment to freeze into immobility the morality dominant at a particular time in a society's existence'. One might as well say that the inclusion of a penal section into a statute prohibiting certain acts freezes the whole statute into immobility and prevents the prohibitions from ever being modified.

These points are elaborated in the sixth lecture at pp. 115-16.

[1] (1951) Cmd. 8190, para. 159.

now sufficient for my purpose. How is the law-maker to ascertain the moral judgements of society? It is surely not enough that they should be reached by the opinion of the majority; it would be too much to require the individual assent of every citizen. English law has evolved and regularly uses a standard which does not depend on the counting of heads. It is that of the reasonable man. He is not to be confused with the rational man. He is not expected to reason about anything and his judgement may be largely a matter of feeling. It is the viewpoint of the man in the street—or to use an archaism familiar to all lawyers—the man in the Clapham omnibus. He might also be called the right-minded man. For my purpose I should like to call him the man in the jury box, for the moral judgement of society must be something about which any twelve men or women drawn at random might after discussion be expected to be unanimous. This was the standard the judges applied in the days before Parliament was as active as it is now and when they laid down rules of public policy. They did not think of themselves as making law but simply as stating principles which every right-minded person would accept as valid. It is what Pollock called 'practical morality', which is based not on theological or philosophical foundations but 'in the mass of continuous experience half-consciously or unconsciously accumulated and embodied in the morality of common sense'. He called it also 'a certain way of thinking on questions of morality which we expect to find in a reasonable civilized man or a reasonable Englishman, taken at random'.[1]

Immorality then, for the purpose of the law, is what every right-minded person is presumed to consider to be immoral. Any immorality is capable of affecting society injuriously and in effect to a greater or lesser extent it usually does; this is what gives the law its *locus standi*. It cannot be shut out. But—and this brings me to the third question—the individual has a *locus standi* too; he cannot be expected to surrender to the judgement of society the whole conduct of his life. It is the old and familiar question of striking a balance between the rights and interests of society and those of the individual. This is something which the law is constantly doing in matters large and small. To take a very down-to-earth example, let me consider the right of the individual whose house adjoins the highway to have access to it; that means in these days the right to have vehicles stationary in the highway, sometimes for a considerable

[1] *Essays in Jurisprudence and Ethics* (1882), Macmillan, pp. 278 and 353.

time if there is a lot of loading or unloading. There are many cases in which the courts have had to balance the private right of access against the public right to use the highway without obstruction. It cannot be done by carving up the highway into public and private areas. It is done by recognizing that each have rights over the whole; that if each were to exercise their rights to the full, they would come into conflict; and therefore that the rights of each must be curtailed so as to ensure as far as possible that the essential needs of each are safeguarded.

I do not think that one can talk sensibly of a public and private morality any more than one can of a public or private highway. Morality is a sphere in which there is a public interest and a private interest, often in conflict, and the problem is to reconcile the two. This does not mean that it is impossible to put forward any general statements about how in our society the balance ought to be struck. Such statements cannot of their nature be rigid or precise; they would not be designed to circumscribe the operation of the law-making power but to guide those who have to apply it. While every decision which a court of law makes when it balances the public against the private interest is an *ad hoc* decision, the cases contain statements of principle to which the court should have regard when it reaches its decision. In the same way it is possible to make general statements of principle which it may be thought the legislature should bear in mind when it is considering the enactment of laws enforcing morals.

I believe that most people would agree upon the chief of these elastic principles. There must be toleration of the maximum individual freedom that is consistent with the integrity of society. It cannot be said that this is a principle that runs all through the criminal law. Much of the criminal law that is regulatory in character —the part of it that deals with *malum prohibitum* rather than *malum in se*—is based upon the opposite principle, that is, that the choice of the individual must give way to the convenience of the many. But in all matters of conscience the principle I have stated is generally held to prevail. It is not confined to thought and speech; it extends to action, as is shown by the recognition of the right to conscientious objection in war-time; this example shows also that conscience will be respected even in times of national danger. The principle appears to me to be peculiarly appropriate to all questions of morals. Nothing should be punished by the law that does not lie beyond the limits of tolerance. It is not nearly enough to say that a majority dislike a practice; there must be a real feeling of reprobation. Those who are dissatisfied with the present law on homosexuality often say that the opponents of reform are swayed simply by disgust. If that were so it would be wrong, but I do not think one can ignore disgust if it is deeply felt and not manufactured. Its presence is a good indication that the bounds of toleration are being reached. Not everything is to be tolerated. No society can do without intolerance, indignation, and disgust;[1] they are the forces behind the moral law, and indeed it can be argued that if they or something like them are not present, the feelings of society cannot be weighty enough to deprive the individual of freedom of choice. I suppose that there is hardly anyone nowadays who would not be disgusted by the thought of deliberate cruelty to animals. No one proposes to relegate that or any other form of sadism to the realm of private morality or to allow it to be practised in public or in private. It would be possible no doubt to point out that until a comparatively short while ago nobody thought very much of cruelty to animals and also that pity and kindliness and the unwillingness to inflict pain are virtues more generally esteemed now than they have ever been in the past. But matters of this sort are not determined by rational argument. Every moral judgement, unless it claims a divine source, is simply a feeling that no right-minded man could behave in any other way without admitting that he was doing wrong. It is the power of a common sense and not the power of reason that is behind the judgements of society. But before a society can put a practice beyond the limits of tolerance there must be a deliberate judgement that the practice is injurious to society. There is, for example, a general abhorrence of homosexuality. We should ask ourselves in the first instance whether, looking at it calmly and dispassionately, we regard it as a vice so abominable that its mere presence is an offence. If that is the genuine feeling of the society in which we live, I do not see how society can be denied the right to eradicate it. Our feeling may not be so intense as that. We may feel about it that, if confined, it is tolerable, but that if it spread it might be gravely injurious; it is in this way that most societies look upon fornication, seeing it as a natural weakness which must be kept within bounds but which cannot be rooted out. It becomes then a question of

[1] These words which have been much criticized, are considered again in the Preface at p. viii.

balance, the danger to society in one scale and the extent of the restriction in the other. On this sort of point the value of an investigation by such a body as the Wolfenden Committee and of its conclusions is manifest.

The limits of tolerance shift. This is supplementary to what I have been saying but of sufficient importance in itself to deserve statement as a separate principle which law-makers have to bear in mind. I suppose that moral standards do not shift; so far as they come from divine revelation they do not, and I am willing to assume that the moral judgements made by a society always remain good for that society. But the extent to which society will tolerate—I mean tolerate, not approve—departures from moral standards varies from generation to generation. It may be that over-all tolerance is always increasing. The pressure of the human mind, always seeking greater freedom of thought, is outwards against the bonds of society forcing their gradual relaxation. It may be that history is a tale of contraction and expansion and that all developed societies are on their way to dissolution. I must not speak of things I do not know; and anyway as a practical matter no society is willing to make provision for its own decay. I return therefore to the simple and observable fact that in matters of morals the limits of tolerance shift. Laws, especially those which are based on morals, are less easily moved. It follows as another good working principle that in any new matter of morals the law should be slow to act. By the next generation the swell of indignation may have abated and the law be left without the strong backing which it needs. But it is then difficult to alter the law without giving the impression that moral judgement is being weakened. This is now one of the factors that is strongly militating against any alteration to the law on homosexuality.

A third elastic principle must be advanced more tentatively. It is that as far as possible privacy should be respected. This is not an idea that has ever been made explicit in the criminal law. Acts or words done or said in public or in private are all brought within its scope without distinction in principle. But there goes with this a strong reluctance on the part of judges and legislators to sanction invasions of privacy in the detection of crime. The police have no more right to trespass than the ordinary citizen has; there is no general right of search; to this extent an Englishman's home is still his castle. The Government is extremely careful in the exercise even of those powers which it claims to be undisputed. Telephone tapping and interference with the mails afford a good illustration of this. A Committee of three Privy Councillors who recently inquired[1] into these activities found that the Home Secretary and his predecessors had already formulated strict rules governing the exercise of these powers and the Committee were able to recommend that they should be continued to be exercised substantially on the same terms. But they reported that the power was 'regarded with general disfavour'.

This indicates a general sentiment that the right to privacy is something to be put in the balance against the enforcement of the law. Ought the same sort of consideration to play any part in the formation of the law? Clearly only in a very limited number of cases. When the help of the law is invoked by an injured citizen, privacy must be irrelevant; the individual cannot ask that his right to privacy should be measured against injury criminally done to another. But when all who are involved in the deed are consenting parties and the injury is done to morals, the public interest in the moral order can be balanced against the claims of privacy. The restriction on police powers of investigation goes further than the affording of a parallel; it means that the detection of crime committed in private and when there is no complaint is bound to be rather haphazard and this is an additional reason for moderation. These considerations do not justify the exclusion of all private immorality from the scope of the law. I think that, as I have already suggested, the test of 'private behaviour' should be substituted for 'private morality' and the influence of the factor should be reduced from that of a definite limitation to that of a matter to be taken into account. Since the gravity of the crime is also a proper consideration, a distinction might well be made in the case of homosexuality between the lesser acts of indecency and the full offence, which on the principles of the Wolfenden Report it would be illogical to do.

The last and the biggest thing to be remembered is that the law is concerned with the minimum and not with the maximum; there is much in the Sermon on the Mount that would be out of place in the Ten Commandments. We all recognize the gap between the moral law and the law of the land. No man is worth much who regulates his conduct with the sole object of escaping punishment, and every worthy society sets for its members standards which are above those of the law. We recognize the existence of such higher standards when we use expressions such as 'moral obligation' and 'morally

[1] (1957) Cmd. 283.

bound'. The distinction was well put in the judgement of African elders in a family dispute: 'We have power to make you divide the crops, for this is our law, and we will see this is done. But we have not power to make you behave like an upright man.'[1]

It can only be because this point is so obvious that it is so frequently ignored. Discussion among law-makers, both professional and amateur, is too often limited to what is right or wrong and good or bad for society. There is a failure to keep separate the two questions I have earlier posed—the question of society's right to pass a moral judgement and the question of whether the arm of the law should be used to enforce the judgement. The criminal law is not a statement of how people ought to behave; it is a statement of what will happen to them if they do not behave; good citizens are not expected to come within reach of it or to set their sights by it, and every enactment should be framed accordingly.

The arm of the law is an instrument to be used by society, and the decision about what particular cases it should be used in is essentially a practical one. Since it is an instrument, it is wise before deciding to use it to have regard to the tools with which it can be fitted and to the machinery which operates it. Its tools are fines, imprisonment, or lesser forms of supervision (such as Borstal and probation) and—not to be ignored—the degradation that often follows upon the publication of the crime. Are any of these suited to the job of dealing with sexual immorality? The fact that there is so much immorality which has never been brought within the law shows that there can be no general rule. It is a matter for decision in each case; but in the case of homosexuality the Wolfenden Report rightly has regard to the views of those who are experienced in dealing with this sort of crime and to those of the clergy who are the natural guardians of public morals.

The machinery which sets the criminal law in motion ends with the verdict and the sentence; and a verdict is given either by magistrates or by a jury. As a general rule, whenever a crime is sufficiently serious to justify a maximum punishment of more than three months, the accused has the right to the verdict of a jury. The result is that magistrates administer mostly what I have called the regulatory part of the law. They deal extensively with drunkenness,

---

[1] A case in the Saa-Katengo Kuta at Lialiu, August 1942, quoted in *The Judicial Process among the Barotse of Northern Rhodesia* by Max Gluckman, Manchester University Press, 1955, p. 172.

gambling, and prostitution, which are matters of morals or close to them, but not with any of the graver moral offences. They are more responsive than juries to the ideas of the legislature; it may not be accidental that the Wolfenden Report, in recommending increased penalties for solicitation, did not go above the limit of three months. Juries tend to dilute the decrees of Parliament with their own ideas of what should be punishable. Their province of course is fact and not law, and I do not mean that they often deliberately disregard the law. But if they think it is too stringent, they sometimes take a very merciful view of the facts. Let me take one example out of many that could be given. It is an offence to have carnal knowledge of a girl under the age of sixteen years. Consent on her part is no defence; if she did not consent, it would of course amount to rape. The law makes special provision for the situation when a boy and girl are near in age. If a man under twenty-four can prove that he had reasonable cause to believe that the girl was over the age of sixteen years, he has a good defence. The law regards the offence as sufficiently serious to make it one that is triable only by a judge at assizes. 'Reasonable cause' means not merely that the boy honestly believed that the girl was over sixteen but also that he must have had reasonable grounds for his belief. In theory it ought not to be an easy defence to make out but in fact it is extremely rare for anyone who advances it to be convicted. The fact is that the girl is often as much to blame as the boy. The object of the law, as judges repeatedly tell juries, is to protect young girls against themselves; but juries are not impressed.

The part that the jury plays in the enforcement of the criminal law, the fact that no grave offence against morals is punishable without their verdict, these are of great importance in relation to the statements of principle that I have been making. They turn what might otherwise be pure exhortation to the legislature into something like rules that the law-makers cannot safely ignore. The man in the jury box is not just an expression; he is an active reality. It will not in the long run work to make laws about morality that are not acceptable to him.

This then is how I believe my third interrogatory should be answered—not by the formulation of hard and fast rules, but by a judgement in each case taking into account the sort of factors I have been mentioning. The line that divides the criminal law from the moral is not determinable by the application of any clear-cut principle. It is like a line that divides land and sea, a coastline of irregularities and indentations. There are gaps and promontories, such as adultery and fornication, which the law has for centuries left substantially untouched. Adultery of the sort that breaks up marriage seems to me to be just as harmful to the social fabric as homosexuality or bigamy. The only ground for putting it outside the criminal law is that a law which made it a crime would be too difficult to enforce; it is too generally regarded as a human weakness not suitably punished by imprisonment. All that the law can do with fornication is to act against its worst manifestations; there is a general abhorrence of the commercialization of vice, and that sentiment gives strength to the law against brothels and immoral earnings. There is no logic to be found in this. The boundary between the criminal law and the moral law is fixed by balancing in the case of each particular crime the pros and cons of legal enforcement in accordance with the sort of considerations I have been outlining. The fact that adultery, fornication, and lesbianism are untouched by the criminal law does not prove that homosexuality ought not to be touched. The error of jurisprudence in the Wolfenden Report is caused by the search for some single principle to explain the division between crime and sin. The Report finds it in the principle that the criminal law exists for the protection of individuals; on this principle fornication in private between consenting adults is outside the law and thus it becomes logically indefensible to bring homosexuality between consenting adults in private within it. But the true principle is that the law exists for the protection of society. It does not discharge its function by protecting the individual from injury, annoyance, corruption, and exploitation; the law must protect also the institutions and the community of ideas, political and moral, without which people cannot live together. Society cannot ignore the morality of the individual any more than it can his loyalty; it flourishes on both and without either it dies.

I have said that the morals which underly the law must be derived from the sense of right and wrong which resides in the community as a whole; it does not matter whence the community of thought comes, whether from one body of doctrine or another or from the knowledge of good and evil which no man is without. If the reasonable man believes that a practice is immoral and believes also —no matter whether the belief is right or wrong, so be it that it is honest and dispassionate—that no right-minded member of his society could think otherwise, then for the purpose of the law it is immoral. This, you may say, makes immorality a question of fact— what the law would consider as self-evident fact no doubt, but still with no higher authority than any other doctrine of public policy. I think that that is so, and indeed the law does not distinguish between an act that is immoral and one that is contrary to public policy. But the law has never yet had occasion to inquire into the differences between Christian morals and those which every right-minded member of society is expected to hold. The inquiry would, I believe, be academic. Moralists would find differences; indeed they would find them between different branches of the Christian faith on subjects such as divorce and birth-control. But for the purpose of the limited entry which the law makes into the field of morals, there is no practical difference. It seems to me therefore that the free-thinker and the non-Christian can accept, without offence to his convictions, the fact that Christian morals are the basis of the criminal law and that he can recognize, also without taking offence, that without the support of the churches the moral order, which has its origin in and takes its strength from Christian beliefs, would collapse.

This brings me back in the end to a question I posed at the beginning. What is the relationship between crime and sin, between the Church and the Law? I do not think that you can equate crime with sin. The divine law and the secular have been disunited, but they are brought together again by the need which each has for the other. It is not my function to emphasize the Church's need of the secular law; it can be put tersely by saying that you cannot have a ceiling without a floor. I am very clear about the law's need for the Church. I have spoken of the criminal law as dealing with the minimum standards of human conduct and the moral law with the maximum. The instrument of the criminal law is punishment; those of the moral law are teaching, training, and exhortation. If the whole dead weight of sin were ever to be allowed to fall upon the law, it could not take the strain. If at any point there is a lack of clear and convincing moral teaching, the administration of the law suffers. Let me take as an illustration of this the law on abortion. I believe that a great many people nowadays do not understand why abortion is wrong. If it is right to prevent conception, at what point does it become sinful to prevent birth and why? I doubt if anyone who has not had a theological training would give a satisfactory answer to that question. Many people regard abortion as the next step when by accident birth-control has failed; and many more people are deterred from abortion not because they think it sinful or illegal but because of the difficulty which illegality puts in the way of obtaining it. The law is powerless to deal with abortion *per se*; unless a tragedy occurs or a 'professional' abortionist is involved—the parallel between the 'professional' in abortions and the 'professional' in fornication is quite close—it has to leave it alone. Without one or other of these features the crime is rarely detected; and when detected, the plea *ad misericordiam* is often too strong. The 'professional' abortionist is usually the unskilled person who for a small reward helps girls in trouble; the man and the girl involved are essential witnesses for the prosecution and therefore go free; the paid abortionist generally receives a very severe sentence, much more severe than that usually given to the paid assistant in immorality, such as the ponce or the brothel-keeper. The reason is because unskilled abortion endangers life. In a case in 1949[1] Lord Chief Justice Goddard said: 'It is because the unskilful attentions of ignorant people in cases of this kind often result in death that attempts to produce abortion are regarded by the law as very serious offences.' This gives the law a twist which disassociates it from morality and, I think, to some extent from sound sense. The act is being punished because it is dangerous, and it is dangerous largely because it is illegal and therefore performed only by the unskilled.

The object of what I have said is not to criticize theology or law in relation to abortion. That is a large subject and beyond my present scope. It is to show what happens to the law in matters of morality about which the community as a whole is not deeply imbued with a sense of sin; the law sags under a weight which it is not constructed to bear and may become permanently warped.

I return now to the main thread of my argument and summarize it. Society cannot live without morals. Its morals are those standards of conduct which the reasonable man approves. A rational man, who is also a good man, may have other standards. If he has no standards at all he is not a good man and need not be further considered. If he has standards, they may be very different; he may, for example, not disapprove of homosexuality or abortion. In that case he will not share in the common morality; but that should not make him deny that it is a social necessity. A rebel may be rational in thinking that

[1] *R. v. Tate, The Times*, 22 June 1949.

he is right but he is irrational if he thinks that society can leave him free to rebel.

A man who concedes that morality is necessary to society must support the use of those instruments without which morality cannot be maintained. The two instruments are those of teaching, which is doctrine, and of enforcement, which is the law. If morals could be taught simply on the basis that they are necessary to society, there would be no social need for religion; it could be left as a purely personal affair. But morality cannot be taught in that way. Loyalty is not taught in that way either. No society has yet solved the problem of how to teach morality without religion. So the law must base itself on Christian morals and to the limit of its ability enforce them, not simply because they are the morals of most of us, nor simply because they are the morals which are taught by the established Church—on these points the law recognizes the right to dissent—but for the compelling reason that without the help of Christian teaching the law will fail.

II

Morals and the Quasi-Criminal Law
and the Law of Tort*

I want here to examine the relationship between, on the one hand, the moral law and, on the other, what I shall call the quasi-criminal law and the civil law of wrongs, that is the law of tort. When I talked in the Maccabaean lecture of crime and sin, I had in mind that part of the criminal law which covers offences *mala in se*. Much of the modern criminal law is concerned with offences that are *mala prohibita*, and this is the part that I call quasi-criminal. The relationship of the moral law to the quasi-criminal law is in my view of it quite different from its relationship to the real criminal law and more like its relationship to the civil law. So I can usefully begin by examining the difference.

In a celebrated passage in his speech in *Donoghue* v. *Stevenson*,[1] Lord Atkin said:

Acts or omissions which any moral code would censure cannot in a practical world be treated so as to give a right to every person injured by them to demand relief. In this way rules of law arise which limit the range of complainants and the extent of their remedy. The rule that you are to love your neighbour becomes in law, you must not injure your neighbour; and the lawyer's question, Who is my neighbour? receives a restricted reply.

Earlier in his speech Lord Atkin spoke of 'a general public senti-ment of moral wrongdoing for which the offender must pay'. The idea that you must not seek without restraint your own profit and well-being but must be careful that in so doing you do not injure others, is a moral idea that is part of the foundation of every good society. This idea provides a moral base for much of the law, civil

---

* The Presidential Address to the Holdsworth Club, delivered at the opening of the new Birmingham University Law Library at Edgbaston, on 17 March 1961.
[1] (1932) A.C. 562 at 580.

and criminal, and in particular for the quasi-criminal law. Some parts of the quasi-criminal law keep closer to the base than others. There are statutes that forbid acts that may be injurious to the health of the community. Then there are statutes like the Food and Drugs Act, designed to protect the public in what they eat, and like the Weights and Measures Act which helps to ensure fair trading. Such statutes may be closely connected with 'the general public sentiment of moral wrongdoing' in that many of the things which they require to be done are the very things which the honest, careful, and considerate citizen should wish to do in the interests of others. At the other extreme there is a statute like the Road and Rail Traffic Act, 1933, which demands of the citizen that he shall not use his vehicle on the roads for the carriage of goods for hire or reward unless he holds in respect of it an 'A' licence. The Act is designed to regulate the flow of goods traffic and to make the best use of roads and vehicles so as to provide an efficient transport system. It aims at an economic rather than a moral target. Even so, in obedience to a law like that there is yet some sort of a moral element. When regulations are made for the economic welfare of the community it may be immoral for a man to obtain, by breaking them, an advantage for himself at the expense of his fellow citizens who accept the restriction. At a time of crisis, when the survival of the nation may depend upon the efficacy of the restriction, this would be generally recognized; but there are also many fussy regulations whose breach it would be pedantic to call immoral.

The distinction between the real criminal law and the quasi-criminal in their relationship to morals is that in the former a moral idea shapes the content of the law and in the latter it provides a base upon which a legal structure can be erected. In the former the law adopts a particular moral idea, usually taken from a divine commandment. In the latter no more is required of the law than that it should maintain contact, more or less remote, with the general moral idea that a man, if he cannot reach the perfection of loving his neighbours, should at least take care not to injure them and should not unfairly snatch an advantage for himself at their expense.

Real crimes are sins with legal definitions. The criminal law is at its best when it sticks closely to the content of the sin. Of course it must trim the edges so that they present a line sharp enough for the clear acquittal or condemnation which the administration of justice requires. There cannot be a theft without an asportation; there must be an intent not merely to take possession of the stolen article but also permanently to deprive the owner thereof; these are the sort of definitions which the temporal law, whose servants cannot enter into the mind of man, requires for its working. The criminal law is at its worst when for ease of enforcement it extends the area of the sin. For centuries past it has done this in the case of murder, constructing synthetic states of mind in substitution for the real intent to kill that makes the sin of murder. But at least there is sin at the heart of the crime.

Quasi-criminal offences are entirely the creature of statute and because of that are sometimes called statutory offences. But the distinction between what is really criminal and what is quasi-criminal is not the distinction between common law and statute law. Nearly all the crimes that originated in the common law are now codified by statute. Many of the statutes that create quasi-criminal offences deal also with real crimes of dishonesty. Thus, the new Weights and Measures Bill s. 16 (2) makes it an offence if any fraud is committed in the use of any weighing equipment. Dishonesty of this sort could probably be brought within one of the old common law crimes; but it was evidently thought to be more convenient that a specific offence should be created which could be dealt with summarily.

The distinguishing mark between the criminal and the quasi-criminal lies not in the use of a special statutory provision but in the presence or absence of moral content in the statutory provision containing the offence. Let me try to explain it by an analogy—a comparison between a citadel and fortified outworks. To protect the sanctity of life against the sins of murder and manslaughter the law builds a citadel. Whatever the sin, it is unlikely that the area enclosed will be no more and no less than the area of the moral principle that has to be protected. This is because the architecture of the law runs in straight lines and at regular angles and thus either something has to be left outside the walls or a plot has to be included to square the enclosure off. I have suggested that, as against the sin of murder, quite a large extra piece has been included, but not enough to destroy the character of the enclosure which remains one that is dominated by a moral principle.

But sometimes the law finds a moral principle too difficult to enclose. Let me take as an example of this the special duty that is owed towards children. An adult can look after himself and must be strong enough in himself to resist temptation; but it is a moral duty to look after a child in this respect and to keep him out of bad ways and not to indulge him unduly. It is impossible to express such a duty in precise terms though it is easy to say how it should be applied to particular cases. There is nothing wrong in giving a child an occasional glass of wine, but it would be quite wrong to give him too much to drink. Most boys have smoked quite a number of cigarettes before they are sixteen but it would be wrong to allow any child to make a regular habit of it. Now, how does the law deal with this situation? All it can do is to build an outpost against the direction from which it thinks danger is most likely to come. So legislation is directed against selling alcohol to children (Licensing Act 1953 s. 128), selling them tobacco (Children and Young Persons Act 1933 s. 7), and allowing them to go into bars (Licensing Act 1953 s. 126). There is nothing in the least immoral in a responsible child buying tobacco for an adult or accompanying his parent into a respectable bar. A child of thirteen could probably take delivery of a pint of bitter in a jug without injury to his moral health. But this class of legislation is justified as the defences which the law throws up to protect a sound moral principle. There is much other legislation of the same sort—restriction upon children taking part in public entertainments (Children and Young Persons Act 1933 s. 22) or having transactions with a marine store dealer (Merchant Shipping Act 1894 s. 540)—a character whom the law has always regarded with exceptional suspicion. All these are punishable offences.

It is in relation to this sort of offence that I use the simile of an outwork. The law by this means seeks, as it were, to prevent the enemy from getting anywhere near his objective; it means that he must be denied admission to territory where he could go without any moral offence at all. Even here the law, so far as the stiffness of its masonry will allow, tries to adapt itself to the ordinary man's notion of propriety. It recognizes, for example, that there may be occasions when 'a person under 14' has to pass through a bar, and so provides that his presence there shall not be an offence if he 'is in the bar solely for the purpose of passing to or from some other part of the premises, not a bar, being a part to or from which there is no other convenient means of access or egress'. It is indeed not easy to translate morality into legal terms!

Even where it constructs a citadel the law may build outposts as well so as to be an added protection. Thus in the Weights and

Measures Bill it is not content with making it an offence for a trader to use a weighing machine dishonestly or to have in his possession for use in trade any weighing machine that is 'false or unjust' (s. 16 (2)). In order to make it difficult for a seller to give short weight and easy for a buyer to detect it, if he does, there are five Schedules of the Bill which will cover twenty-six pages of the Statute book requiring in respect of innumerable categories of goods that they should 'be sold only by quantity expressed in a particular manner or only in a particular quantity' (s. 23). If you can surround a citadel with a system of outworks of this sort you may prevent the enemy from even approaching the walls that defend honest trading.

The first distinguishing mark of the quasi-criminal law then, is that a breach of it does not mean that the offender has done anything morally wrong. The second distinguishing mark is that the law frequently does not care whether it catches the actual offender or not. Owners of goods are frequently made absolutely liable for what happens to the goods while they are under their control even if they are in no way responsible for the interference; an example is when food is contaminated or adulterated. Likewise, they may be made liable for the acts of their agents even if they have expressly forbidden the act which caused the offence. This sort of measure can be justified by the argument that it induces persons in charge of an organization to take steps to see that the law is enforced in respect of things under their control. In most cases it is simply a mild form of collective punishment. In some of our colonies where the police force is sparse and the population scattered, and the detection of crime exceptionally difficult, the law provides for imposing a collective fine on a village where there has been disorderly behaviour. That helps to ensure that the inhabitants will keep order among themselves. In England a more refined form of vicarious liability prevails. The majority of quasi-criminal offences are committed in the course of trade or commerce and the fines that are imposed in respect of them fall upon the shareholders of a limited company or the proprietors of the business.

It is, I think, a pity that the distinction between the criminal and the quasi-criminal, the *mala in se* and the *mala prohibita*, has become blurred. According to the Austinian theory of law, which, although it has lost influence in academic circles, still retains its grip upon many practising lawyers who imbibed it when they were young, the distinction does not exist. The force of law is to be derived simply from the power to command obedience and no distinction is to be drawn between the commandment 'Thou shalt not kill' and the commandment 'Thou shalt not drive on the right of the road'. For myself, I find the theory advanced by Dr. Goodhart much more satisfying.[1] Following in the steps of Sir Frederick Pollock, he regards the force behind the law as the citizen's sense of obligation. The sense of obligation which leads the citizen to obey a law that is good in itself is, I think, different in quality from that which leads to obedience to a regulation designed to secure a good end. In the first the judgement of the State and the citizen on what is good and what is evil should coincide and so obedience to the law is an end in itself; in obeying it the citizen is doing a good thing. In the second their judgement that the end is good should coincide but their judgement on the efficacy and propriety of the means chosen to serve that end need not coincide. Frequently it does not, but the citizen accepts that the choice of means must be left to the State and for that reason will obey a law that he may think very silly.

It is a pity that this distinction, which I believe the ordinary man readily recognizes, is not acknowledged in the administration of justice. The lack of an overt distinction has damaged the law. It would have damaged it far more than it has were it not that the ordinary man still retains the distinction in his mind; he still thinks of the word 'crime' as disgraceful or morally wrong. But he cannot be expected to go on doing so for ever if the law jumbles morals and sanitary regulations together and teaches him to have no more respect for the Ten Commandments than for the wood-working regulations. Meanwhile, so long as the distinction still means something to the ordinary man it may cause him unnecessary distress if for some petty offence which he may not even himself have committed, he is classed among criminals and if in the machinery of the law he is processed as if he were one. There is in truth no reason why the quasi-criminal should be treated with any more ignominy than a man who has incurred a penalty for failing to return a library book in time.[2]

---

[1] *English Law and the Moral Law*, 1953, p. 18.

[2] This distinction has been criticized by Lady Wootton in *Crime and the Criminal Law*, pp. 41 et seq.

She regards the argument as 'circular'. As she puts it, real crime is defined as an offence that the good citizen does not commit without a sense of guilt; and the good citizen is defined as someone who would not commit what the definer believes to be a real crime without feeling guilty about it. If the definer believes in old established

The distinction between *mala in se* and *mala prohibita*, if it could be revived and clarified, might play a useful part in constitutional law. It has for centuries past been a principle of the constitution that a man should not be imprisoned unless he be condemned by his countrymen. During the last hundred years encroachments on this principle have been allowed. It has, I think, become important to establish as a convention a clearer line than that which exists at present to mark the boundary beyond which any further invasion

---

morality he will call any breach of it a 'real crime'; and the distinction will simply be a stockade to protect old crimes—*mala antiqua* as Lady Wootton puts it—from the wind of change.

I do not think that the test should be subjective. There is a large number of offences which no one, unless he is amoral, can commit without a sense of guilt, irrespective of whether he is likely to be detected and punished for it. Broadly speaking, these are offences against the moral law. There is also a large number of offences which a person with a highly developed moral sense can commit without any sense of guilt at all and where the only deterrent is the penalty that he would have to pay. Most of the crimes in the calendar could, I think, by general agreement be assigned to one or other of these categories. Undoubtedly there would be a number about which opinions will differ. But if the normal in one type is distinguishable from the normal in the other and the two types can with advantage be given separate treatment, it is not a valid objection to separation that there will be variations from type and borderline cases. Some division between major and minor crimes has always been a feature of our criminal law. The division between felonies and misdemeanours was useful until it was allowed to become archaic. In modern times the division is between those crimes which are grave enough to entitle the accused to trial by jury and those which can be disposed of summarily. A division based on the gravity of the crime is not susceptible of exact definition and the same is true of a division based on common morality.

But on the basis, which I assume at this stage, that there is a common morality generally accepted, what I suggest is that a division which takes morality as a guide will strengthen morality by treating it as a distinguishing factor and strengthen the law by enlisting the ordinary man's sense of guilt in support of its weightier provisions.

The distinction, as Lady Wootton readily recognizes, does not lie simply between *nova* and *antiqua*. Motoring offences are novel only in the sense that motors are a recent invention. There is nothing novel about the idea of condemning the deliberate or reckless use of a dangerous instrument, whether it is a battle-axe, a gun, a motor-car, or a deleterious foodstuff. What is novel is the idea of condemning a man who is not personally responsible for its use and who neither did nor could reasonably be expected to foresee the harm that was done. Age is not the same as obsolescence. If most of our existing morality is antique, as it is, it is because the sense of right and wrong does not fundamentally change very much.

Lady Wootton considers that the criminal law should not be used punitively but only preventively. There should be a number of forbidden acts and any person who commits one will break the criminal law; but his state of mind when doing the act should be irrelevant to the question of whether or not it is criminal, because he is not going to be punished for it but only prevented from doing it again. On this theory there is of course no room for any distinction between criminal and quasi-criminal law. It is too large a subject for a footnote.

should not go. Let me endeavour to show the part the distinction might play in this.

The basis for the distinction between *mala in se* and *mala prohibita*, between what one might call a crime and an offence—or between what one might call a felony and a misdemeanour, if one could modernize those terms so that the latter was given its natural meaning—is that crime means to the ordinary man something that is sinful or immoral, and an offence at worst a piece of misbehaviour. A jury is a good tribunal for trying crime in that sense because it handles naturally issues involving moral guilt. It is not so effective for trying breaches of good order and discipline where every juryman can identify himself too readily with the accused. An offence that does not involve moral guilt rarely calls for serious punishment. Offences against the State, such as treason and sedition, and wilful and continued defiance of the law may call for serious punishment, but I regard them also as offences against morals. That may be controversial; but at least they are offences against society of the same gravity as moral offences because they strike at the health and life of society. They are *mala in se*. If we renewed the distinction between *mala in se* and *mala prohibita* and if it were accepted, as I think it should be, that in a civilized society the former are properly punishable by imprisonment and that the latter generally are not; and if we confine the jury to its traditional role, as laid down in the Magna Carta,[1] of safeguarding the liberty of the person, we should build a strong defence against the tyranny of the State. Let the State have a regulated power over the purse of the citizen and support it with the aid of the magistracy, but let it have no power over his body unless it can persuade his fellow countrymen to deprive him of his liberty.

We may think now that we begin to perceive a gradient leading from the depths of the criminal to the heights of the moral law. Gross and deliberate breaches of the moral law that are deeply injurious to society are corporally punished. Disregard of social obligations is also punishable though more mildly; thereby the secular law comes nearer to the precept that a man should act, if not with love towards his neighbour, at least not without consideration. The civil law, one might suppose, should come nearer still; for it contains no penal provisions and so ought to be able to regulate

[1] ... *nullus liber homo capiatur, vel imprisonetur* ... *nisi per legale judicium parium suorum.*

the conduct of one man towards another without that attraction towards the minimum that must inevitably be felt by a law which is prescribing what is punishable.

But that is not the way in which the law of tort has grown up nor is it the function which it now performs. Normally the relevant question in this branch of the law is not 'Who is to blame?' but 'Who is to pay if things go wrong?'; and the judgement is expressed as a sum fixed not as punishment for blameworthiness but as compensation for damage done. I do not think that a branch of the law whose object is to provide compensation for damage can be used directly to serve a moral purpose. The reason, put shortly, is that while liability can be made to depend upon moral guilt, full compensation for injury done cannot be made to depend on the *degree* of moral guilt: guilt depends upon a state of mind but damage done does not. But for the moment let me put that difficulty on one side and consider to what extent liability in the law of tort depends upon moral guilt. That is tantamount to asking what part is played in the law of tort by malice or the deliberate intent to injure, or by negligence sufficiently gross to constitute a moral fault. We all know that negligence in some degree, great or small, plays a considerable part: malice on the other hand as an element in liability has, except in a few specific torts, a very small part to play. I shall begin by considering negligence.

Much of English law, both civil and criminal, originated as rules for payment for wrong done, blameworthiness being irrelevant. At a very early stage the concept of *mens rea*, or the guilty mind, was introduced into the criminal law and thereafter a man was not punished unless he had acted deliberately or at least with gross recklessness. The rules for compensation were left to the civil law and for a long time these were based on absolute liability. A man trespassed at his peril on the person or property of his neighbour; he was liable even though he had no idea that he was trespassing. Likewise, he created or kept at his peril sources of danger or nuisance, such as fire, wild beasts, and accumulations of water; if they got out of control, he was liable whether he was careless or not. These liabilities were and still are separately classified as specific torts. The big chance came when all the large area left uncategorized was partly filled with the tort of negligence. The creation and development of that tort was not deliberately designed to serve a moral purpose. But because its efficacy depended upon proof of a state of mind, the state of carelessness, it had, as *mens rea* had on the criminal law though to a much more limited extent, a fertilizing influence upon the civil law and brought it into contact with moral fault. It affected not only the uncategorized area which it helped to fill, but the classified torts as well. The area of absolute liability for physical injury at common law has now dwindled almost to nothing. The elastic concept of negligence enables liability to be graded to fit the circumstances. The greater the risk of injury the greater the care that must be taken. When the danger is high, then, as Lord Macmillan put it in *Donoghue* v. *Stevenson*,[1] 'the law exacts a degree of diligence so stringent as to amount practically to a guarantee of safety'. Even the ancient torts of trespass and assault may be beginning to yield to this treatment.[2]

But there is also another influence upon the law of tort which has been flowing in the opposite direction. In the important field of industrial injury the common law has been stiffened by statute. The Factories Acts and the mass of regulations made under them go a long way towards making the employer absolutely liable for accidents occurring in the handling of machinery or as a result of factory conditions or of the special dangers that arise in the course of particular operations such as building. This does not mean that the legislature adopted the view that an employer was morally bound to pay, irrespective of fault, for injuries arising out of employment and decided to take a step towards that end. The Acts were passed as part of the quasi-criminal law; their object was to diminish the number of industrial accidents by prescribing rigid precautions and punishing the employer if they were not taken, whether the fault was his or another's. They became part of the civil law by virtue of the common law doctrine that if an Act of Parliament is considered by the Courts to have been passed not merely as a matter of public order but for the protection of individual members of the public, a man hurt by its breach, may, notwithstanding that the Act itself is criminal in form and prescribes only penalties for the breach of it, recover compensation from the wrongdoer. The Factories Acts are now far more important as a source of civil law than as part of the quasi-criminal law: minor infringements, too slight to give rise to

---

[1] (1932), A.C. 562, at 611.

[2] See the discussion in Pollock on *Torts* (15th edn.), p. 128, and since then *National Coal Board* v. *Evans* (1951), 2 K.B.861, *Fowler* v. *Lanning* (1959), 1 Q.B. 426, and *Letang* v. *Cooper* (1964), 2 A.E.R. 929.

prosecution, are constantly invoked in actions brought by work-men. The common law is letting out absolute liability by one door and bringing it in by another, but all without any conscious purpose.

Another factor bringing negligence and absolute liability closer together is the change that has taken place in the standard of care. It is becoming much stricter than it used to be. Almost any departure from the high standard that is set for the prudent man is sufficient to sustain a claim, and not infrequently a judge consoles a defendant by telling him that while he—it would generally be truer to say his insurance company—must pay for his error, he need not regard himself as morally to blame. Negligence in law ranges from in-advertence that is hardly more than accidental to sinful disregard of the safety of others. When Rolfe B., in his celebrated dictum[1] said that gross negligence was only negligence with the addition of a vituperative epithet, it was tantamount to saying that in the law of negligence moral fault was irrelevant.

One way or another, either by way of absolute liability or upon proof of negligence, the English law of tort provides compre-hensively for physical injury. The tort of negligence fills the gaps that would otherwise have existed between specific torts, but only between those such as assault and trespass which are based on physical injury. It can be taken as a general principle that if a man ought to foresee that his act will probably cause injury to the person or property of another and he does not take proper care to avoid that consequence, he will be liable. No general principle of the same sort covers injury to another's purse or reputation. In that field the law of tort retains unaltered its primitive form of division into specific categories, each with its own characteristics. Some, like defamation, retain absolute liability as the basis. In libel and slander there need be no intent to injure reputation; a fiction writer who accidentally portrays an unpleasant character that can be mistaken for a living person is liable. In the common law of libel negligence has no part to play: statute has recently given it a limited application. Under the common law a man was absolutely liable if he distributed a newspaper containing libellous matter of which he was entirely ignorant, but the Defamation Act of 1952 has modified that. Other torts, such as fraud and malicious prosecution, depend upon proof of a guilty mind. There must be an intention to injure and carelessness

[1] *Wilson v. Bratt* (1873), 11 M. & W. 115.

is not enough. As the law at present stands,[1] a man has no redress for a careless statement made to him personally which causes him to act in a way that injures him financially even if the maker of the statement actually foresaw that he would so act, unless there is between them some special relationship, such as that of a solicitor and his client, created by contract or otherwise. There is no general duty to take care not to cause financial loss to another.

The influence of malice (the law includes within that term any wilful intent to injure as well as a malicious or spiteful state of mind) is much smaller than negligence. Where physical injury is done, there is no need for it since negligence is wider. In the case of other types of injury malice is, as I have already mentioned, an ingredient in some specific torts: but that is all. There is a tort of negligence but no tort of malice; and as for malice as an ingredient in other torts, the general rule is that either the act is unlawful without malice or it is not unlawful at all. This feature shows more clearly than any other the nature of the English law of tort; that it is grounded on absolute liability, in parts overlaid and in parts modified by the concept of negligence: that is almost all there is to it. If the mental element in the law of tort had not been an afterthought, malice could never have been deemed almost wholly irrelevant. In this respect English law contrasts unhappily with the law in those countries, such as France and Germany, where there is a civil code.[2]

Apart from the four specific torts, there are two ways by which malice enters the law of tort, one by way of the common law and the other by way of equity. The former operates through the law of damages. There is power to award punitive damages in a limited class of torts, of which the chief are defamation, assault, and seduction. The law departs from its normal rule that it is irrelevant to the amount of damages whether the injury was caused deliberately or accidentally, and permits an award in excess of the true compensation for injury done so as to punish the defendant for his malice and express indignation at the outrage done to the plaintiff. This is not very satisfactory either in principle or in practice. In principle there is no good moral reason why an injured person should make a profit out of another's vice. Sometimes the profit is enormous. A

[1] But the law on this point does not now stand precisely where it stood in 1961. If the principles enunciated in *Hedley Byrne* v. *Heller* (1964) A.C. 465, are further developed, they should go a long way towards removing what later in this lecture (p. 41) I refer to as 'the great blemish on the law of tort'.

[2] See Lawson, *Rational Strength of English Law*, 1951, pp. 115 and 116.

sum large enough to punish a wealthy newspaper may be a small fortune (free of tax) for a libelled person. A soiled reputation often rates in the courts much more money than a crippled limb. In practice such awards are not coolly assessed. They are almost invariably made by a jury without time for reflection and maybe in a gust of indignation—perhaps caused by the defence tactics at the trial if they have not come off, for that can be taken into consideration. *Loudon* v. *Ryder*[1] is an example of a case in which a jury awarded an enormous sum for quite trivial injuries. There was a dispute between a mother and a daughter about the ownership of a flat and a male friend of the mother's invaded the flat in an attempt to turn the daughter out. In the course of this he struck her on the shoulders and head. It was an outrageous thing to do, but no real injury was inflicted; and apart from some nervous shock no harm was done. The jury awarded her £5,500 damages. This was no modern development for in the course of the hearing a case was referred to in 1814 in which the judge said that he remembered a case where a jury gave £500 damages for merely knocking a man's hat off.

The other way in which malice is relevant comes from equity and, as in the case of punitive damages, its field of operation is limited. A plaintiff, whatever his motives, can get damages if his rights are infringed, but he cannot get as of right the equitable remedies of injunction and specific performance. These superior remedies are not often appropriate anyway—they are drastic and could be used, for example, to make a defendant pull down a building if it transgressed the boundary line—but they will never be granted if asked for out of spite.

This brief survey of the scope allowed in the law of tort for malice and negligence shows, I think, that while moral forces have been at work in shaping parts of it, the law as a whole is without any consistent moral purpose. It does not stand in an auxiliary relationship to the moral law. Is not that inevitable, one may ask. The object of this branch of the law is to repair injury, usually by means of money; its chief sanction is the judgement for damages and that is

[1] (1953), 2 Q.B. 202. This case has now been overruled by *Rookes* v. *Barnard* (1964), A.C. 1129. It is unlikely that any practitioner will pick up a book such as this in order to obtain information about the law on punitive damages. But if by any chance he has done so, he should be warned that the observations of Lord Devlin in *Rookes* v. *Barnard*, with which the other Lords agreed, will now afford more reliable guidance than the statement in the text.

not a weapon that can conveniently be used for a moral purpose. It cannot, as can a fine, be adjusted to the means of the offender; nor on the other hand does it always reflect the enormity of the injury. It is, for example, cheaper to kill than to maim; for dead men cease to suffer and the Courts, in despair of doing justice, have fixed a nominal sum as compensation for loss of expectation of life. But almost invariably a sum awarded as damages is far higher than the fine which would be imposed in respect of the same act if it were treated as a crime—out of all proportion higher, so that if the real object was as a punishment or deterrent, it would be immoral and unjust because so crushing. In fact in England the real wrong-doer hardly ever pays for the damage he does. He is not usually worth suing. The payer is either his employer or his insurance company. As a rule the only sanction which the law of tort enforces against a man who is morally guilty is the possibility of disfavour in the eyes of his employer or the probability that his insurance premium will be increased.

I conclude therefore that it is wrong to regard the law of tort as associated with the criminal and quasi-criminal law in the work of promoting good standards of behaviour in the community. An illusion that there is a close association of this sort is largely created by the name given—torts or wrongs—to this branch of the law. 'The words "tort" and "tortious" have perhaps a somewhat sinister sound but, particularly where the tort is not deliberate but is an act of negligence, it does not seem that there is any more moral obliquity in it than in a perhaps deliberate breach of contract.'[1]

It is true that some torts are sins; deceit is an obvious example, but generally speaking in the civil law legal wrongdoing is quite a different concept from moral wrongdoing. Malice or wilfulness or gross negligence (not just the sort of inadvertence that often is enough to amount to negligence in law) is an essential element in moral wrongdoing; it may or may not have to be present in a tort, and whether it is a necessary ingredient or not can be learnt only from an examination of that particular tort and does not depend on general principle. Most tortfeasors are innocent of any moral offence. The fact is that the law of tort is not generally concerned with behaviour. Its attitude is: 'You can do what you like so long as you pay for it.' Its function is to decide how and by whom, in the absence of agreement, damage is to be made good. There is no need for it to perform any

---

[1] Viscount Simonds in *The Wagon Mound*, (1961) A.C. 388 at 420.

other function. If an injury done to another involves social mis-behaviour, it can be dealt with under the criminal or quasi-criminal law with a penalty commensurate to the degree of moral blame; if it does not, the doing of the injury does not infringe the moral law.

But this does not mean that because the law of tort is not to be regarded as an adjunct of the moral law in the sense that the criminal law and the quasi-criminal law are, its provisions are immune from test by moral standards. Its relationship to morality is much more casual but is not wholly detached. The question whether a man should pay for the damage done to another is one which can be—and frequently is, especially in the smaller affairs of life which are not litigated—settled as a matter of morals. 'You ought to make that good' or 'You are morally bound to pay for that' are common expressions showing that without the assistance of the law the ordinary man has an idea of what justice requires. When he uses such expressions, he is not necessarily condemning the other man for having done something wrongful; he is merely saying how a loss ought to be adjusted. The law of tort, as the branch of the law which is concerned with that adjustment, ought to be in accord with the ordinary man's sense of justice. Granted all that I have said about the effect of insurance and vicarious liability in diverting the payment for the loss from the pocket of the person who has actually caused it, there remains a sound sentiment that a person who has without good excuse caused loss ought to be held liable for it and an equally sound sentiment that there are injuries which ought to be redressed as well, maybe, as punished.

This is not saying much more than that justice is a moral idea. It would not, morally speaking, be satisfactory simply to say that it does not matter which side, the active or the passive, pays for the loss so long as there is a rule that makes it clear in advance on whom the loss is going to fall. There is, not invariably but frequently, a right and a wrong about who should pay for a loss. That is what makes moral justice and it should be the target of legal justice.

But this branch of the law is more remote than usual from moral justice. Ideally there are only two forces that need separate the secular and the moral law. The first is the need of the former for a greater degree of rigidity and uniformity: the legal judgement has to express itself with greater precision than is needed for a moral judgement and cannot, since it may be used as a precedent, afford to pay the same attention to individual circumstances. The second is that the secular law, because its function is to impose a sanction, must be framed to comply with lower standards than those aimed at by the moral law. The first of these forces operates with unusual strength when questions of compensation arise, particularly when the act giving rise to them is accidental or inadvertent. For example, the means of the parties will properly be taken into account by a moralist. It might be thought as wrong for a rich man to refuse to compensate a poor man for an accident which he brought about as it would be for a rich man in a similar case to exact compensation which might be the ruin of a poor man; but the notion of responsibility based on what a man can afford cannot easily be introduced into a code of legal liability. In many cases with which the law of tort has to deal, the only moral principle that can be invoked is that a man ought according to his means to do his best to help a neighbour in misfortune, together with the sentimental addendum that the obligation should weigh especially heavily on him if any act of his, innocent or not, has contributed to the misfortune.

There are many principles in the law of tort which, if they touch morality at all, raise questions that are unlikely to get the same answer from all moralists. Should a master always be responsible for the acts of his servants? Should an employer be absolutely liable to his employees for accidents in the course of their employment? If a man keeps a dog, ought he to be liable for any harm it does? The moral law provides no universal answer to such questions. The utmost that can be expected from the law of tort is that no part of it ought to be positively repugnant to the ordinary man's sense of moral justice, because it is from that that all law draws its strength. That is the only point at which the law of tort comes into contact with the moral law and subject to that it is free to make its own rules.

Judged in this way, how does the English law of tort appear? I do not regard it as a blemish that absolute liability still plays a substantial part in it. It is usual to think of absolute liability as a primitive idea which the superior notion of liability based on negligence is gradually driving out of the common law. But absolute liability is not *per se* morally bad; there is nothing immoral about the idea that there are acts which a man does at his peril in the sense that if they go wrong he must pay for the consequences. To my mind the great blemish on the law of tort is its failure to provide adequately for injury other than physical done maliciously or carelessly. This seems to me to be due simply to under-development. The concept of negligence has been exploited up to a point, but has not apparently retained sufficient of its initial impetus to jump the barrier between the corporeal and the incorporeal. The concept of malice is hardly used at all. This deficiency affects not only the jurisprudential quality of the law of tort but creates an unnecessarily wide gap between the law of tort and the moral law. It leaves far too large an area of culpable injury without redress and far too many cases in which the good citizen should feel under a moral obligation which the law does not enforce.

To my mind the law of tort is the least satisfactory branch of English law. It may not be accidental that it is also the one which of its nature has least to do with morals. The criminal law is shaped by the moral law; the quasi-criminal is based on it; the law of contract is the legal expression of the moral idea of good faith; the law of divorce formulates the permissible relaxations from the moral ideal of the sacramental marriage. The judges of England have rarely been original thinkers or great jurists. They have been craftsmen rather than creators. They have needed the stuff of morals to be supplied to them so that out of it they could fashion law; when they have had to make their own stuff their work is inferior.

III

Morals and the Law of Contract*

That there is a relationship between the law of England and the
moral law is a proposition which no one can sensibly deny. Whether
there ought to be such a relationship is another matter. Some people
believe that the law need not have any moral content at all and that
the moral content which in fact it has is hampering to its development. On this view the moral law should be something private to
the individual which he determines for himself; and the civil law,
i.e., the law of the land, should consist of regulations made for the
good order and discipline of society. English law did not originate
in that way and I doubt whether the law of any society in which
religious beliefs are held is born as a set of club rules. For where
there is religious belief, there is also a belief in the right and wrong
way of doing things and the formulation of the law on any point
takes its start from that. In its development many other factors,
shaped to suit convenience only, play a part. Some branches of the
law have a much larger moral content than others but I do not think
that there is any branch of English law that is quite without it.

Those who think that the law of the land should concern itself
only with order and regulation are naturally indifferent to its moral
content which for them is just a matter of legal history. For others,
who value the connexion between law and morality, it is a profitable
exercise to overhaul from time to time a branch of the law, to identify
and restate the moral principles that lie behind it, and to see how
effective the law is in promoting and applying them. It is in this spirit
that I want to make a brief survey of the English law of contract.

The moralist cannot say much more about contract than that the
good man should keep faith and deal fairly. The pragmatist, if I may
affix that label for want of a better to those who are concerned only to
see that the law regulates the activities of the members of society

* A lecture delivered at the Queen's University of Belfast on 2 March 1962.

where they impinge on one another, would say that there is no need to talk in moral terms about keeping faith; whether keeping faith is good or bad for the soul is something that each man can decide for himself. All that society need say about it is that as a matter of convenience a man must stick to his bargain, for otherwise social relations would not be possible.

In all legal systems both these ideas find their expression to a greater or less degree in the law of contract. The development of English contract law has favoured the pragmatic rather than the moral. This is not, I think, because the English were less influenced by moral considerations than other nations, but because at the time when the common law was growing they were more interested than others in commerce and so the common law of contract was designed mainly to serve commerce. If a man minded only about keeping faith, the spirit of the contract would be more important than the letter. But in the service of commerce the letter is in many ways the more significant. This is because in most commercial contracts many more than the original parties are concerned. The contract is embodied in a document which may pass from hand to hand when the goods it represents are sold over and over again to a string of buyers, or when money is borrowed on it, or insurances arranged. The spirit of the contract gets lost on these travels and the outward form is all that matters. For the common law the sanctity of the contract means the sanctity of the written word in the form in which it is ultimately enshrined. Normally, evidence is not admissible of conversations or correspondence leading up to the contract; they cannot be used to amplify or modify the final document. That document must speak for itself. For the common law has its eye fixed as closely on the third man as on the original parties; and the final document is the only thing that can speak to the third man.

For the same reason, that is, because of the effect on third parties, the common law is very reluctant to allow a contract that looks good to be vitiated by a flaw in the making of it. It does not require full disclosure and *caveat emptor* is the general rule. There is only one case in which the full disclosure that good faith would prompt is required by the common law and it is noteworthy that this is to satisfy the commercial needs of underwriters in the contract of insurance. The contract of insurance is *uberrimae fidei*, i.e., demanding the utmost good faith. But the common law has been concerned to make it clear that in this type of contract the requirement of good faith does not rest on any general principle; underwriters are presumed to require full disclosure as a condition of the contract.[1]

If there is a mistake in the making of a contract, the common law does not make it easy to get relief from it. If the contract is induced by misrepresentation, the common law will give relief if it amounts to a lie, but not if it was made innocently, even though with a complete lack of care. If a party wants to rely on a representation, the common law says, let him make it a warranty, put it in the contract and not leave it to wander about outside where the third man cannot see it. Likewise indeed, all the terms that are wanted should be expressed in the contract. If one is not, it must be apparent to the third man—the officious bystander, as Lord Justice McKinnon has called him[2]—that it is needed before it can be implied.

The common law will not concern itself with motive for a breach of contract. In many branches of trade, for example, it is well understood that if between the making of the contract and the delivery of the goods the market has moved against a party, that party will scrutinize the performance very closely to see if there is not some minute falling short that would entitle him to reject the goods. That he should do so is quite in accordance with the common law which does not care whether the breach is accidental or deliberate. Whether it is perfidious and dishonourable or due to sheer misfortune, the consequences are just the same.

Equity came into existence as the first response of the law to the complaint that the justice it administered was failing to give effect to moral obligations that were generally recognized. Equity treated good faith as an obligation to be imposed by the law of its own motion; it did not resort, as the common law did in the case of the contract of insurance, to the fiction that it was an implied term of the contract. It declared that there were certain relationships, which it called fiduciary relationships, in which complete good faith must be observed. Partnership is one. The relation of an agent to his principal and of a solicitor to his client are others. Such relationships cannot be fruitful if they are conducted on the footing that each side is seeking to outwit the other as in a business bargain.

Thus equity softened the crudities of the common law. It dealt less strictly with mistake and misrepresentation. In other ways it has influenced the law of contract indirectly. Take the case of the man

---

[1] *William Pickersgill* v. *London Insurance* (1912) 3 K.B. 614 at 621.
[2] *Shirlaw* v. *Southern Foundries* (1939) 2 K.B. 206 at 227.

who has led the other party to the contract to believe that he is not going to insist strictly on a term of his contract. The common law, left to itself, would be inclined to say that the only question was whether he made a binding promise not to insist. But this is not now the law. If, for example, the delivery date in a contract has not been met and the buyer nevertheless keeps pressing for the goods, he cannot when at last they are delivered reject them on the ground that they are out of time. He is taken to have waived the delivery date and if he wants to bring back a time limit into the contract, he must make a new delivery date by giving the seller reasonable time within which to deliver the goods. This doctrine, which appears under various guises such as forbearance, waiver, and quasi-estoppel and stretches at least from *Jones* v. *Gibbon* in 1853[1] to the *Hightrees* case in 1947,[2] is generally ascribed to equitable influence.

But good faith flowing out of equity is still the exception rather than the rule in the law of contract. In most systems of law, the French and German for example,[3] the requirement of good faith in the performance of the contract is a general one, not exceptional as in the English. Yet as Professor Powell has shown, the general requirement tends to be systematized into a series of rules. The breaking down of a general principle and its confinement to certain categories may in the end produce much the same result as the categorization of exceptions, though the two processes start from opposite extremes. Legalization is in one sense the natural enemy of morality, for morality is at its best when each case is judged entirely on its individual merits; provided always that the judge is a good judge. So in another sense law is the friend and servant of morality, for by translating it into rules, even though thereby its edge is blunted, its administration is protected from the aberrations of the judge. The rules should be proof not against the winds of change but against the gusts of prejudice. Making the rules weather-proof is an important service that law renders to morality. There is danger in a general requirement of good faith. The general requirement in the German code was used during the Nazi régime to support the false morality that no one could in good faith deal with Jews.[4]

---

[1] 8 Ex. 920.   [2] (1947) 1 K.B. 130.

[3] See article 1134 of the French code and s.157 of the German code and the consideration of them by Professor Powell in his lecture 'Good Faith in Contracts', *Current Legal Problems*, 1956, p. 16.

[4] Powell, op. cit. citing Dr. Cohn.

I have been talking of equity and good faith. I think that perhaps the greater service that equity rendered to the law of contract was in assisting the second of the two moral principles I have mentioned, the principle of fair dealing. The two principles are so intertwined that it is perhaps unwise to try to separate them. But though they can often be used to give the same answer to the same question, essentially they embody different ideas. Good faith demands complete honesty in the making and fulfilment of the bargain. But it does not prevent the bargain from being a harsh one nor put a brake upon its strict enforcement. Fair dealing demands that the stronger or cleverer party shall not try to subdue or outwit the other in the making of the contract; and that a man shall not exercise arbitrarily the power given him by the contract but treat it as something to be used only to secure fulfilment of the contractual purpose. The common lawyers hardly regarded the principle of fair dealing as one that needed independent support. For them free dealing was fair dealing. So long as fraud and deceit were kept out of the ring, it was up to each party to fight for the best bargain he could get; a fair fight meant that a fair bargain would result.

In business negotiations where the parties are equally matched, this is broadly true. If the Court were to interfere otherwise than as a referee to prevent fouls, or if it were to tender help to the party who appeared to be getting the worst of it, worse still if it engaged itself as an active promoter of fair dealing, sooner or later it would be telling both parties that it knew what was good for them better than they did themselves. That is an attitude that always has been and still is repugnant to lawyers of every persuasion, equitable as well as common. 'The Chancery mends no man's bargain' said Lord Chancellor Nottingham in 1676.[1] Equity, before it will redress the balance in an individual case, must be shown some inequality in status which, so to speak, rebuts the presumption of fair dealing on which the common law operates. Such an inequality might come from a relationship between the parties which was likely to give to one party an undue influence over the other; or it might spring from the circumstances of a particular case, a rich and worldly-wise man dealing with a poor and ignorant one. Inevitably the recipients of equity tended to fall more and more into classes, the administrators of equity grew more and more reluctant to add to the

---

[1] *Maynard* v. *Moseley*, 3 Swan 651 at 655.

classification, and with the conquest of poverty and the spread of education the numbers in existing classes have diminished. One class, to which equity was especially tender, that of expectant heirs, has been decimated by the conquest of riches.

The same process of classification has affected the broad principle that equity will intervene to prevent a man from using his contractual powers in a harsh or oppressive way. Mortgagees as a class have the equity of redemption and tenants get relief against forfeiture. All forfeiture clauses and penalty clauses are abhorrent to equity, notwithstanding that they are voluntarily entered into, for they allow a man not merely to reimburse himself what he has lost by another's breach of contract but also to enrich himself at the expense, maybe, of another's misfortune. Such a use of the power of forfeiture is deemed to be harsh and unconscionable. 'Unconscionable' is the great word. Equity does not want to stop good business being done but it tries to prevent sharp practice and oppression.

Whether the general principle can still be expanded outside the recognized classes is a matter of current judicial controversy. It is no longer true, Lord Justice Harman has recently said,[1] that the Chancellor still has only the length of his own foot to measure when coming to a conclusion. But the boot that once encased the Lord Chancellor's foot is now sported by a commoner leg and equitable principles are being bandied about in common law courts. While the common lawyers, notably Lord Denning, seek to squeeze at least a trickle from a source that might have fertilized the whole field of contract, the Chancery declares that the system of equity was fossilized in the time of Lord Eldon.

The consequence is that the legislature has taken up the task which equity left unfinished. The protection of the weak is now undertaken by statute and the weapon used is more often destruction than reform, the statute prohibiting altogether the making of the contract. Statute of its nature works by classification. The most striking example of a class for which equity did nothing and which is now the darling of the legislature is that of the manual worker. For most of the nineteenth century a workman was in no position to bargain with his employer and the relationship of master and servant was one of the first, and still is one of the largest, of the fields which Parliament has entered so as to protect the weaker side. The first

[1] *Campbell Discount* v. *Bridge* (1961) 1 Q.B. 445 at 458. Compare this with the speech of Lord Denning (1962) A.C. 600 at 629.

Truck Act was passed in 1831. Since then there have been the Workmen's Compensation Acts and the Factory Acts among many others. It would take too long even to catalogue all the classes of contracts that are now regulated by bodies of statute law. The Rent Acts and statutes controlling hire-purchase and moneylending are some examples among many.

There is one sort of contract, much used today, that has been left largely untouched both by equity and by statute. If the modern lawyer had to single out the type of contract which now bears most marks of oppressive and unfair dealing, I think he would probably select one contained in the mass of small print which the large concern thrusts upon the small man in a 'take it or leave it' way. The small print contains and conceals every sort of exemption from liability which the ingenuity of the form-monger can devise. The common law holds tightly to the conception of the reasonable man as one who peruses every word of the contract before signing it. Since judges are not often entirely ignorant of the facts of life it is necessary to keep the judicial tongue well tucked into the judicial cheek when enunciating this principle. Consistently with it the most the common law can do to help is when the contractual document is unsigned, as when one is given a railway ticket. Then exceptions will not be binding unless enough is done to bring them to the notice of the recipient. Sometimes, but not often, the legislature takes a hand as in the case of carriage of goods by railway, by laying down standard conditions which are deemed to be fair to both sides. The same result is achieved when both sides belong to powerful organizations and can hammer out an agreed form.

It is the ordinary citizen who is oppressed. If the reasonable man 'worked to rule' by perusing to the point of comprehension every form he was handed, the commercial and administrative life of the country would creep to a standstill. The ordinary citizen is ill-equipped to do battle on a field of unpunctuated clauses and strewn with legal jargon. But what is worse is that if he wants to do battle it is only with great difficulty that he can find anyone to do it with. The man behind the counter has not the slightest idea what is in the form nor the man behind him nor the man behind the managing director's desk. Their weapons are shrugs and soothing words. It is only in some alley-way leading to a remote back room that the campaigner would come up against the closed door on which is written 'Take it or leave it'.

All this seems on the face of it most oppressive. But on reflection I doubt whether there is a moral issue involved. What the men behind the form-monger really want to achieve is not so much exemption from liability as exemption from litigation. They do not really want to line their pockets with the money that should go to compensate those whom their goods or activities have maimed or impoverished; they want to judge for themselves what claims they should meet. They like to act through the *ex gratia* payment. Whether they are prompted by a conscience that makes them recognize the moral duty to make good the harm they or their servants do or by a desire not to deter potential customers does not go to the point I am considering. Their incomprehension of the maxim '*nemo debet esse judex in propria sua causa*'[1] is deplorable but not immoral. The contractual rubbish they concoct (it is not often examined; it is generally left in the bin; it is not meant to stand up to scrutiny so much as to deter litigation) is a social nuisance rather than a moral evil. Indeed, since in the modern state the capitalist can no longer grow rich on the sufferings of the poor, the whole thing is an economic rather than a moral problem. Which is better: to be fully compensated if the pilot of your aircraft is negligent or to have a pound or so knocked off the price of your seat and be your own insurer? Morality has no answer to this problem. It is a matter of convenience, and often, as in the case of air travel, the legislature steps in with a compromise. The Warsaw Convention enforced in this country by the Carriage by Air Act, 1932, allows a modicum to be recovered from the carrier and for the rest the passenger must protect himself.

It is not possible to say that a contract is oppressive simply by looking at the exception clauses; you must look at the contract as a whole. This is what Mr. Justice Blackburn said in 1863: 'I think that a condition exempting the carriers wholly from liability for the neglect and default of their servants is *prima facie* unreasonable. I do not go so far as to say that it is necessarily in every case unreasonable and void. A carrier is bound to carry for a reasonable remuneration, and if he offers to do so, but at the same time offers in the alternative to carry on the terms that he shall have no liability at all, and holds forth as an inducement a reduction of the price below that which would be reasonable remuneration for carrying at carriers' risk, or some additional advantage, which he is not bound to give, to those that employ him with a common law liability, I think

[1] 'No one ought to be a judge in his own cause.'

that a condition thus offered may be reasonable enough.' This was said in a case that arose under the Railway and Canal Traffic Act, 1854.[1] That Act was passed because railways were then using their superior bargaining power to impose what terms they wanted on their customers; and, broadly speaking, it provided that conditions designed to relieve the companies of their ordinary liabilities must be 'just and reasonable'. Today standard terms and conditions are settled by the Transport Tribunal and they reflect the distinction which Mr. Justice Blackburn drew. There are rates for goods carried at owners' risk and higher rates for those carried at carriers' risk. No one can complain about that.

The Railway Act of 1854 was a comparatively early example of statutory intervention in the field of contract. The intervention was made not by prohibiting contracts which the legislature disliked or by laying down rigid terms but by a general and flexible provision that the contract must be fair and reasonable. You may think it a pity that Parliament does not use this sort of provision more. But, as I have said, it is not one which, at any rate since medieval times, the law of England has cared for at all. Judges do not mind saying what is reasonable provided that it is something that can be expressed in figures, such as a reasonable price or reasonable time. But they object to saying what is fair, for that, they say, would be making a contract. They will allow an arbitrator to say what is fair—though they view it with suspicion; 'the Cadi under the palm tree', Lord Justice Scrutton called him—provided the parties say quite clearly what they want him to do. This seems sensible enough. I do not see why a man should be discouraged from saying that if certain contingencies arise, he simply wants to do what may be thought in the circumstances to be fair and reasonable; a law that forbade him to do that would itself be unfair and unreasonable. But when it comes to making the terms, it is better that it should be done by a person of his own selection—a business man if it be a business contract—rather than by a lawyer.

The English law of contract is then a hotch-potch of the common law, equity, and statute. Taken as a whole it is biased in favour of commerce rather than morality. It should be easy to devise a workable system that goes further than the English law does in the promotion of good faith and fair dealing. It suffers from trying to do too much with one set of principles. There are so many varieties of

[1] *Peek* v. *North Staffordshire Railway* (1863), 10 H.L.C. 473 at 511.

contract that it would be difficult to find principles that are well adapted for them all. In business a man will act with an astuteness that he would scorn to exercise in private affairs.

On the other hand it can be argued that since there must be a gap between the way in which the good man should aim to behave and the way in which the law makes him behave, there is something to be said for letting the law of contract as a general rule take its tone from the business contract and for leaving it to the individual to set himself a higher standard in gentler relationships. And even in commerce no one can say that the common law has bred in the average business man any lack of concern for good faith. Sometimes indeed he can make the lawyer blush. I remember once at the Bar having to negotiate the settlement of a case in which the client had plainly broken his contract and the only question was the amount of damages he should pay. The other side were prepared to accept a sum that I thought less than what they might well have demanded, but they insisted on a formal document in which my client admitted the paragraphs in the statement of claim which contained the allegations of breach of contract. When I put this to my client, he refused. I pointed out that he obviously had broken the contract and we argued about it for some time. At last he said: 'Oh, I see what you mean. That I have failed to comply with my contract. I don't mind admitting that. That might happen to anyone. But I have never committed a breach of contract in my life.'

I turn now to another question that always arises when the relationship between the moral law and any branch of the civil law is being considered. Only the criminal law can be used to enforce moral standards; but it can be asked of other branches of the law that they should at least reflect society's disapproval of any immorality that the criminal law does not condemn. Obviously, the law cannot specifically enforce contracts requiring the performance of acts which the law itself forbids to be done. English law extends this embargo to acts which although not contrary to law are contrary to morality, such as fornication. The courts will not enforce a covenant to provide for a mistress. A landlord who discovers his lodgers are living in sin must turn them out or else rely on their sense of honour for the rent. But English law goes further than this. It treats such contracts not merely as unenforceable but as suffering from an infectious disease. It will not even help a man who has acted on the faith of them to get what in justice is his due.

No one, I think, can doubt that this is the right principle to apply to acts which are really criminal or immoral. You cannot imagine the courts entertaining an action for damages for failing to commit a murder as agreed; and the same rule must apply against a man who seeks to recover a payment made in advance for a murder that the payee failed to commit. One has more sympathy with a discarded mistress who seeks to recover the money she was promised. It may be pleaded that even sinners are entitled to justice; but then it may be answered that morality is affronted if the courts are used to distribute the wages of sin and that if they were, moral standards would inevitably be weakened. At any rate, no one who accepts that the law is concerned with morality can quarrel with it if, on such matters, it tends to take a rigid stand.

But the principle should I think be confined to the direct consequences of the wicked act. The hardship that can be caused if it is allowed to operate beyond that is illuminated by *Amicable Society* v. *Bolland*.[1] One would have thought that even in 1830 death would have been considered a sufficient punishment for forgery and that the law need not add to it by depriving the dead man's dependants of the benefits secured for them under a policy made long before. Mr. Fauntleroy insured his life in January 1815 and regularly paid the premium of £128 15s. a year until October 1824, when he was tried and convicted for forgery, sentenced to death, and executed on 30 November 1824. What was it that destroyed the policy, counsel for the beneficiaries inquired. Not the felonious act, for that had happened long before and many premiums had thereafter been taken. Not even the conviction, for, as he ingeniously argued, if Fauntleroy instead of being hanged, had been transported and the ship lost, his death would not have voided the policy. 'Fauntleroy meant to do wrong', he conceded, 'but he did not mean to be hanged.' But the House of Lords—or rather the Lord Chancellor; for the argument did not attract a great attendance and there appears to have been present besides the Lord Chancellor only one earl who had, the Lord Chancellor said, 'listened with the utmost attention to the argument at the Bar'[2]—held that the suit could

---

[1] (1830), 2 Dow & Clark 1.
[2] ibid. at 20. Quite probably the noble earl had. He was the third Earl of Radnor, the friend of Alexis de Tocqueville, whom he took to see the Salisbury justices at petty sessions. See de Tocqueville's *Journeys to England and Ireland*, ed. J. P. Mayer, Faber and Faber, London, 1958.

not be maintained, for if the policy were not held void, it would afford an encouragement to crime.

This wholesale condemnation of illegality, instead of promoting morality, frequently encourages roguery. This has happened even when the initial object of the law was a highly moral one, particularly perhaps when it was too highly moral. Take gaming and wagering. Excessive gambling may be immoral—certainly it is socially undesirable—and there may be people who regard even the placing of a single small bet as sinful. But in England gaming and wagering have never been generally condemned as immoral. The common law was quite happy to entertain actions about bets 'provided it was not against the interest or feelings of third parties and did not lead to indecent evidence and was not contrary to public policy'.[1] The laws against gaming depend on statute.

Suing for the payment of a bet is not like suing for the proceeds of a crime. The Royal Commission on Betting[2] thought that the courts ought not to be burdened with such claims and in any event I daresay the public would find other tribunals more satisfactorily constituted for determining who won the 3.30. But there is nothing shocking in an action on a bet. Certainly there is nothing shocking in the idea that a man should be made to honour a cheque which he has given for betting debts. On the contrary it is rather shocking that the law should, as it does, allow a bilker to get away with it. It might well be thought desirable that there should be some restrictive legislation so that book-makers like money-lenders, are prevented from battening on the follies of others, but that is another matter.

Betting is in quite a different category from really criminal activities. Book-makers and punters could not without the grossest hypocrisy be denied admission to the courts on the grounds that justice is not a commodity available for sinners. So the reason for their outlawry is presumably the hope that people are deterred from betting by the thought that the law will not help them to recover their winnings. If that be the object it is surely time to recognize that it has failed lamentably. It is a sufficient commentary on the ordinary man's attitude to the law on this point that he calls debts of the sort which the law ignores 'debts of honour'.

Betting is something that is at least capable of attracting moral disapproval. So much cannot be said of the mass of minor prohibitions

---

[1] *Chitty on Contracts*, 22nd edn., vol. 2, p. 601.
[2] (1951), Cmd. 8190, para. 447.

which constitute the quasi–criminal law. All governments now find it necessary to regulate the daily lives of their subjects by telling them what they must not do and putting a penalty on their doing it; and if sometimes they seem to act as if regimentation was an end in itself, this is not the place to complain about that. But what, one may ask, has the law of contract got to do with it? Of course if Parliament says that a particular class of contract is not to be made, the courts cannot treat such contracts as if they were good. But the great mass of these social prohibitions is not directly against the making of contracts as such but against the doing of acts. Such acts may or may not involve incidentally the making of a contract. A man who carries goods in an unlicensed vehicle may be carrying his own goods or the goods of another for reward; in the former case there is no contract involved, in the latter there is. So a man who builds a house which costs more than the licensed figure is probably, but not necessarily, building under contract. For the offences which they have committed the statute itself will prescribe the appropriate penalty.

What reason is there to suppose that the statute intends also that the carrier or the builder should not be paid for the work he has done? If his wrongdoing deprives him of the payment he has earned, his punishment becomes quite arbitrary. The sum he loses may be a little or a lot; it may be a hundred times or more the maximum fine that could be imposed. Whatever it is, it is not collected for the benefit of the State but it is left in the pockets of the other party who may himself have instigated the breach of the law. 'The Court must enforce the prohibition even though the person breaking the law relies upon his own illegality.'[1] This dictum of Lord Justice Scrutton was made in a case in which the man who was successful in getting out of his contract had deceived the other party by pretending that he had a licence to trade when he had not. So the innocent man, who could not even have known that he was offending, was punished and the wicked was helped on his way. The principle that the law does not aid the wrongdoer is at best only a procedural maxim, for it is true in law as well as in life that often the best way of helping one side is to do nothing for the other.

These legal attitudes promote neither morality nor obedience to the law. On the contrary they shock the conscience and reward knavery. It says much for the English moral character that there has

[1] *Re Mahmoud* (1921), 2 K.B. 716 at 729.

not grown up a class of footpads whose expertise it is to find their way through the morass of quasi-criminal legislation and to make their living out of pushing others into it.

Much of the legal doctrine on this subject is based on the notion that it is the duty of the courts, whenever Parliament passes a statute to regulate an activity, to consider what contracts it must by implication have intended to make illegal. If Parliament wants to make a contract illegal, cannot it say so? Need judges, as if they were sycophants who have to anticipate their masters' wishes even before they are uttered, be so zealous in smelling out new victims and devising further punishments? Yet for a hundred years and more the judges have been grappling with the task of trying to find out what Parliament meant by what it did not say; and not unnaturally have left a confused trail of cases behind them.

Ought a man to be made to pay for his tobacco if he has bought it from a dealer, who has not, as required by statute, had painted on his business premises his name in letters publicly visible and legible and at least an inch long and not more than three feet from the top of the door? The answer is, yes, he ought, but only after a long argument.[1]

In 1824 a certain Mr. Bloxsome had a narrow escape from being seriously out of pocket.[2] The Lord's Day Observance Act had undoubtedly a high moral purpose and it provided among other things that any person who did the 'work of their ordinary calling upon the Lord's Day' must forfeit five shillings. Mr. Bloxsome was travelling in Berkshire on a Sunday and he took a fancy to one of the horses of a stage coach and bought it from the coach proprietor, Mr. Williams, for thirty-nine guineas. Mr. Williams warranted the horse to be sound and not more than seven years old and it was delivered and paid for on the following Tuesday. When Mr. Bloxsome discovered that the horse was far from sound and seventeen years old, he naturally wanted his money back. But the Lord's Day Observance Act placed unexpected difficulties in his path because Mr. Williams was not only a coach proprietor but also a horse-dealer and so was carrying on the work of his ordinary calling on the Lord's day. Mr. Bloxsome successfully evaded the effects of the statute by ingeniously arguing that the bargain was not concluded until the Tuesday, since on the Sunday there was no note or memo-

[1] *Smith* v. *Mawhood* (1845), 14 M. & W. 52.
[2] *Bloxsome* v. *Williams*, 3 B. & C. 232.

randum of it sufficient to satisfy the Statute of Frauds. But apart from that, the judge held, Mr. Bloxsome could have got his money back in any event because he did not know that Mr. Williams was a horse-dealer. Had he known that, and nevertheless in his desire for the horse flung morality to the winds, he could not have recovered; and Mr. Williams would have had a very profitable Sabbath since for a penalty of five shillings he would have sold a worthless horse for thirty-nine guineas.

Two years before, in 1822, a Mr. Bensley had been less fortunate.[1] For the sum of £92 5s. he printed a pamphlet for a Mr. Bignold. But then Bignold found himself unable or unwilling to pay for the printing. Fortunately for him Bensley had omitted to put his proper name on the pamphlet as required by statute under a penalty of £20. So the printer was not allowed to enforce his contract and the pamphleteer got the work done for nothing. In effect Bensley was fined £72 5s. more than the maximum.

Sometimes the courts in their anxiety to trip up the malefactor with red tape allow themselves to become more legislative-minded than the legislative, to adapt a famous phrase.[2] There is a stuff known to the trade that deals in it as 'salvage'. It consists of the sweepings from the holds of ships that have carried cargoes of fertilizers. In *Anderson* v *Daniels*[3] the plaintiff sold ten tons of the stuff for £77. The Fertilizers Act 1906 required that the seller of fertilizers should give to the purchaser an invoice with the analysis of the article sold. It was agreed that in the case of sweepings such an analysis would either be entirely impracticable or absurdly expensive in relation to the price of salvage. So it was the custom of the trade to sell fertilizers without analyses. The custom no doubt worked well enough until there came a buyer who did not want to pay for the goods he had had. So the plaintiff, in addition to as much of the maximum penalty of £20 as the magistrates may have thought appropriate for the gravity of the offence, lost his £77. But in this case the servants of the law had run farther and faster than their masters intended; and no more than the usual amount of parliamentary time was lost in overturning the decision. The Fertilizers Act 1927, section 1(2), enacted that failure to give a statutory statement in accordance with the provisions of the section should not invalidate a contract for sale.

---

[1] *Bensley* v. *Bignold*, 5 B. & Ald. 335.
[2] 'Judges who show themselves more executive minded than the executive.' Lord Atkin in *Liversidge* v. *Anderson* (1942) A.C. 206 at 244.   [3] (1924) 1 K.B. 138.

In *Marles* v. *Philip Trent Ltd.*[1] the same thing happened in the case of some seeds. Seed merchants sold to a farmer some wheat seed. They failed to supply him with a statement in writing showing that the seed satisfied the requirements as to purity and germination laid down by the Seeds Act 1920. This did not trouble the farmer because in fact the merchants had had the seed tested and it did satisfy the requirements. What did trouble him was that his crop failed; and it failed because the seed was sold to him as spring wheat when in fact it was winter wheat. So he brought an action for breach of warranty and recovered £418 5s. 10d. and costs. Then the merchants sued their supplier because he had sold the seed to them as spring wheat. The supplier had no defence to a breach of warranty. But what he said was that the merchants could not recover the £418 as damages because it was damages awarded against them for breach of an illegal contract; they had not supplied the farmer with a statement in writing about purity and germination (which of course had nothing to do with whether the seed was spring wheat or winter wheat). The suppliers won on this point and so the merchants were out of pocket to the tune of £418 and costs. The maximum penalty for their failure to supply the statement was £5. Parliament took only about a year to repudiate this consequence of its supposed intentions. The decision was given on 16 February 1953, and the Act nullifying it, the Agriculture Act 1954, received the royal assent on 4 June 1954. Section 12(1) provides that the validity of a contract for the sale of seeds or the right to enforce it shall not be affected by any illegality under the Seeds Act in the performance of the contract.

The principles which these cases illustrate are now too firmly embedded in the common law to be excised by anything short of legislation, either piecemeal legislation of the sort of which I have just given examples, or something more comprehensive which tries to settle matters of principle. One may at least hope that the defence of illegality will not be extended. I should like to think that there has been a tendency in recent years to scrutinize carefully this type of defence and to recognize that the injustice which it occasions in individual cases may be too high a price to pay for the purification of the law courts.[2]

---

[1] (1954), 1 Q.B. 29.
[2] *St. John Corporation* v. *Joseph Rank Ltd.* (1954) 1 Q.B. 267 at 288 and *Archbolds* v. *Spenglett* (1961) 1 Q.B. 374.

Where there is something more than mere illegality, that is, where the illegality amounts also to a breach of the moral law, the position is different. Even then the dominant principle should be that the courts of justice are open to all, to wrongdoers as well as to the virtuous. The thief and the prostitute do not *ipso facto* put themselves beyond the pale. The rule should be that everyone is entitled to his just deserts whether he has broken the law or kept it. The exception can be justified only when some other high purpose of society, higher than the grant of justice in the individual case, has to be served. When the grant of justice would cause public scandal, the merits of the individual case must yield to the necessities of the law. The law needs moral support and in return it must be prepared to support public morality; and where that would be outraged by the use of law, then, but only then, the law should refuse its aid.

The refusal of aid will not be effective unless there is a strong moral sentiment already at work. The prohibition of contracts and the denial of relief in connexion with matters that are not generally regarded as reprehensible, even though as in the case of gambling they may contain a tincture of immorality, is futile. The law of contract can be used as an auxiliary force but cannot provide the main power. Its force is defensive rather than aggressive. The justification for its use is that the public display of litigation about vice in the course of the daily business of the courts and its reception at the seat of justice on the same terms as virtue would weaken the respect on which moral standards depend.

The principle has now been allowed to spread far beyond the Latin in which it was originally contained. *Ex dolo malo*, it is sometimes said, *non oritur actio*. Or sometimes *ex turpi causa*. Or sometimes *ex maleficio*. *Dolus* is guile and *dolus malus* is the guile that deceives or cheats. *Turpis* is base and shameful. *Maleficium*, Dr. Broom says, means 'an act radically vicious and illegal'.[1] These are the maxims from which the rule was drawn and the judicial language in which it used to be applied employs the same exalted terminology. 'You shall not stipulate for iniquity', Lord Chief Justice Wilmot declaimed in 1767.[2] 'No polluted hand shall touch the pure fountains of justice. . . . *Procul, O! procul este profani*', and so forth. The majestic confluence of English and Latin has now overflowed the banks and such wretched *profani* as failed to deliver the right

---

[1] *Broom's Legal Maxims*, 10th edn., p. 501.
[2] *Collins* v. *Blantern* (1767), *Smith's Leading Cases*, 13th edn., 406 at 411.

sort of invoices get caught up in the flood. When the failure is due
to accident, negligence, or simple ignorance of the regulation, they
surely do not deserve to be drowned. But suppose that they positively stipulate for iniquity? Suppose that they are so lost to legal right-
mindedness as to say to each other: 'To hell with the invoice.'
Well, suppose they do. Let them then be mulcted to the uttermost
in the penalty that Parliament has prescribed. But to nullify the
contract and allow the loss to lie where it falls is to impose an
arbitrary and often excessive punishment which the astute may with
luck avoid, leaving the unwary to suffer. Let it be left to the legislature that has made the crime to make also the punishment to fit it.

You may feel perhaps that I have gone further than my subject
should have taken me in concerning myself with the law's attitude
to illegality as distinct from immorality. I believe not. It is not merely
that the denial of justice except for good and sufficient reason is in a
general sense an offence against morality. I can be more particular
than that. The doctrine *ex turpi causa* has made its way into the law
as an extension of a moral principle. If it is misused, the principle
suffers. Moreover, its misuse is a symptom of a disease of thought
that debilitates the law and morals. This is the failure to recognize
that there is a fundamental difference between the law that expresses
a moral principle and the law that is only a social regulation. If
only in the growth of English law that distinction had been maintained, much of the arbitrariness and the absurdities in the cases I
have cited would have been avoided. There is a dictum of Lord
Wright's which may some day be used as a foundation for a change
of heart. Speaking of the maxim *ex turpi causa*, he said: 'In these
days there are many statutory offences which are the subject of the
criminal law and in that sense are crimes, but which would, it
seems, afford no moral justification for a court to apply the maxim.'[1]

---

[1] *Beresford* v. *Royal Insurance* (1937), 2 K.B. at 220.

IV

Morals and the Law of Marriage*

In the regulation of marriage and divorce the secular law is bound more closely to the moral law than in any other subject. This is quite natural. The institution of marriage is the creation of morality. The moral law of a society is made up from the ideas which members of that society have in common about the right way to live. The association of man and woman in wedlock has from time immemorial been of such importance in every society that its regulation has always been a matter of morals. Whether the union should be monogamous or polygamous, whether it should be dissoluble or not, and what obligations the spouses should undertake towards each other are not questions which any society has ever left to individuals to settle for themselves. They must be settled according to the ideas of right and wrong which prevail in that society, that is, according to its moral law; and because the institution of marriage is fundamental to society the moral law regulates it very closely—much more closely than in most other subjects in which the moral and secular law both operate. In ordinary contract, for example, morality has not much more to say than that bargains should be made in good faith and fairly kept. Beyond that the secular law is left free to devise a set of rules intended to make contract a useful instrument in the conduct of the citizen's affairs. But for almost every detail of matrimony the moral law prescribes a right and wrong. This makes it very easy to find a basis for an examination of the relationship between the secular law of marriage and divorce and the moral law. The law of the land has no function other than to give such aid as is thought necessary or helpful from the secular arm.

I believe that what I have just said will command universal assent provided that morality is not confounded with religion. That is an equation which the law-maker in this country is not permitted

* The Earl Grey Memorial Lecture delivered at the University of Durham on 15 March 1963.

to make.[1] It is the complaint of many agnostics and free-thinkers that in fact this confusion lies at the root of our divorce law. Of course, the whole of our moral law is religious in origin and we talk of the sort of marriage which is recognized in this country as 'Christian marriage'. No sensible person, however anti-religious he may be, will suggest that we should scrap the whole of our moral law as having objectionable origins. Wherever the ideas come from, they now form the community's notion of good and evil. What the sensible free-thinker can properly demand is that only those canons of good and evil which still are generally obeyed should be taken as the basis of the secular law. The law must be taken from present and not from past morality and cannot be justified simply on the basis that it accords with Christian doctrine. Until a few centuries ago, the moral as well as the religious idea of Christian marriage was that it was indissoluble. Indeed, a suggestion that there might be a moral idea of marriage to be contrasted with a religious one would have been incomprehensible to the people of that time. There are still many Christians who regard marriage as absolutely indissoluble and it is very possible that as a matter of Christian doctrine they are right. But if they were to seek to have that idea embodied in the law of the land, they would have to rely upon doctrine and not upon morals. It is no longer generally thought in this country to be morally wrong that a marriage should be dissolved and the spouses freed to marry again.

It is of course absurd to suppose that agnosticism or atheism inevitably produce moral laxity or that either necessarily breeds indifference to the value of the marriage bond. The sensible free-thinker accepts that marriage is a fundamental institution in any society and that society has a right to lay down the conditions under which it should be recognized. In this country he accepts also that it should be monogamous. Monogamy is so deeply rooted in our moral ideas that it would not be practicable to contend that the secular law should recognize any other form. But apart from that, the free-thinker in western civilization would, I believe, accept monogamy as good in itself. Polygamy or polyandry must result in the degradation of either the man or the woman below the level of

---

[1] 'It is, I hope, unnecessary to say that the court is perfectly impartial in matters of religion, for the reason that it has as a court no evidence, no knowledge, no views as to the respective merits of the religious views of various denominations.' per Scrutton L. J. in re Carroll (1931) 1 K.B. 317 at 336.

dignity which according to western ideas is deemed to be his or her right. He would accept also as inherently sound the Christian idea of the spouses' duty towards one another. It is essential that they should live together, that they should cherish and support one another, sharing each other's fortunes and providing the foundation for a family if that is to come. It is also essential to monogamy that there should be sexual fidelity. The consequence of an infidelity, whether it should be treated as mortal to the marriage or as venial, may be a matter for argument but some obligation there must be. For with promiscuity monogamy would degenerate into unregulated polygamy.

In short, the right-thinking man in western society accepts a Christian notion of marriage as the ideal and would not dispute that the secular law should be based upon it. His real complaint is, I think, that when it comes to formulate the terms on which a marriage is dissoluble, the secular law still subordinates itself to outmoded doctrine. That is one of the matters I shall have to consider.

The secular law must be made for unbelievers since it does not require religious belief as a condition of citizenship and exacts compliance from the religious and the irreligious. What the law has to assist are the moral ideas of the good man who is free to think as he likes. I believe that fundamentally Christian marriage does commend itself to such a man. Consequently the object of the secular law should be to do what it can to enable Christian marriage to function well and to give of its best to society. Is English law so framed as to achieve that object?

I shall divide the object into three. First, the law must provide for the terms of marriage: how it is to be made and how ended and what the obligations of the spouses are to be. This would be necessary even if the terms of the marriage concerned only the parties themselves. Most ordinary contracts are of no concern to the public. Nevertheless there has to be a law of contract to provide a basis on which the parties can impose their particular arrangement. If the law did not render this service to the citizen, the making of a contract without provision in it for every contingency would be intolerably laborious. The service should be especially welcome in the case of marriage, for courtship and legal draftsmanship are unnatural companions. Moreover, the terms of a marriage are not of purely private concern. Marriage, though entered into by contract, confers, when completed, a status in society and that gives society a say in the terms of the arrangement. The law must therefore settle all the main terms of marriage, and it must settle also the relationship between the spouses and third parties, which cannot be the same as if the spouses were two disunited individuals.

In the second category—perhaps it should really come first but I think that I shall make myself clearer if I take it second—the law must prescribe the conditions under which entry into marriage is permitted or licensed. Under this head there comes the most controversial question of all, namely, the conditions under which the State should permit a second marriage when the other party to the first is still alive.

Finally, since the modern State concerns itself with promoting institutions which are beneficial to society, the legislator has to consider how the law can best be used to help marriage and to discourage alternatives. This is largely a sociological matter outside the scope of this lecture but there is one relevant aspect of it which in due course I shall note.

The bulk of this lecture however is concerned with the first two categories; and I must begin by answering an obvious inquiry—why it is that I have distinguished between them. English law, it can be pointed out, does not so distinguish. It is true that English matrimonial law is now made up out of a mixture of the common law, equity, and the old ecclesiastical law; but none of these, either in their separate parts or in their modern composition, distinguishes between the obligations of marriage as one subject and the entry into marriage and its dissolution as another and different subject. This distinction is fundamental to my argument and I must occupy a little time in expounding it. I do not think that it is possible to understand the defects of the present law nor how they can be remedied unless it is appreciated. Put into concrete terms, it is the distinction between the decree of judicial separation and the decree of divorce. The State provides courts of law to regulate the affairs of partners as between themselves and with third parties, to determine disputes between them, to wind up their affairs when the partnership is dissolved and to divide the property between them, and so forth. The State must provide in the same way for the regulation and determination of a marriage and that is what it is doing up to the point when the court grants a decree of judicial separation. That is the physical divorce, the winding up of the partnership and the absolution of one partner from the obligation of living with the other. This is what was called, until 1857 when modern divorce law began, the divorce *a mensa et thoro*, from the table and the hearth, the physical divorce.

But when it goes beyond that and grants the divorce *a vinculi*, it is venturing into an entirely different territory. What is the bond which it is purporting then to break? Not a temporal or physical bond. All that it can do temporally and physically it does with the decree of judicial separation. By that decree the court relieves the parties completely from the temporal and physical obligations of marriage. Thereafter they need no longer live together or support or provide for each other as man and wife. When a temporal court has so decreed, it has exhausted its powers. How, in a country in which no one is compelled to believe in any religion, can the State assume power to dissolve a spiritual bond as distinct from a temporal obligation? It is absurd to suppose that the State can either make or unmake marriage. For those who believe in the sacrament that can be done only by God; and for those who do not so believe, it can be done only by the parties themselves. All that the State can do is to register their decision. The State does not claim to make marriages, only to recognize and register them; and likewise it can register no more than their physical and temporal conclusion.

The extraordinary notion that a judge of the Probate, Divorce and Admiralty Division of the High Court, who may be a man of any religion or none, is, when not engaged on Probate or Admiralty business, invested with spiritual powers, comes out of a typically English confusion of ecclesiastical and lay jurisdictions. Before 1857 suits for judicial separation were brought before the ecclesiastical courts because all matters pertaining to marriage belonged to them. But it was only because the State recognized and enforced the decrees of the ecclesiastical courts that these had any temporal effect. There was no anomaly when in 1857 this jurisdiction was taken over by the temporal courts—rather the reverse.

The ecclesiastical courts never pronounced the decree *a vinculi*. They very nearly did so and at one time after the Reformation it was thought that they would. But in the end it was left to Parliament to enact the bill of divorcement and thereby to assume a spiritual function. In 1857 Parliament transferred its own powers as well as those of the ecclesiastical courts to the newly constituted Probate, Divorce and Admiralty Division of the High Court. Was Parliament aware that it was transferring a mixture of the spiritual and the temporal? Did it consider what the requisites for a spiritual court are? The decrees of a spiritual court are binding only upon conscience and as such they are effective because the belief of the parties who are subject to the decree requires them to submit their decision to that of the court. If these beliefs are not held by the suitors before the court, it is wasting its time. In 1857 Parliament could have believed that the State and the Established Church were still so connected in the minds of Englishmen that they would not distinguish between spiritual and temporal jurisdictions and would submit their consciences to a lay judge. A century later it is not possible to believe that. What then is the divorce court really doing when it pronounces a decree of divorce? What is it doing, that is to say, over and above the decree of judicial separation? What it is really doing is to permit remarriage. The State, as I have said, cannot make or unmake marriage but it can recognize or refuse to recognize marriage. What the State is doing when it pronounces a decree of divorce is saying that it will recognize any other marriage that either party chooses to make. That is the practical effect—indeed it is the only effect, unless it is supposed that the court has spiritual powers—of the decree.

I shall have to consider the effect on the development of our matrimonial law of this confusion between the temporal and the spiritual. I have, I hope, said enough at this stage to justify the distinction I have drawn between the first and second categories. In the second category the interest of the State is dominant. In the first category, which I must now examine, the interest of the State is subordinate and the inquiry is to ascertain how far the law of the land in dealing with the obligation of the spouses, severally towards each other and jointly towards outsiders, corresponds with modern morality and whether or not it is now unduly influenced by its religious source.

There is not much common law on this subject because until 1857 it was mainly within the jurisdiction of the ecclesiastical courts. The law now administered by the secular courts is the old ecclesiastical law embodied in statute and with modern statutory additions, but in its structure it is similar to the ordinary law of contract. Firstly, the conditions essential to the validity of the contract are laid down. Secondly, the shape and obligations of the contract are prescribed. Thirdly, remedies are given for breach of obligations. I doubt if a new law-maker, concerned only with secular values, would want to demolish this structure and begin again. Ought he, if he were firmly resolved to eliminate everything that could justify its place only by an appeal to religious doctrine, to make any substantial alterations to the content of the law under any of these three heads?

Under the first head there are the usual sort of provisions designed to secure that the contract is entered into freely and voluntarily and by persons who are capable of performing its obligations. There is also the usual sort of confusion common throughout English legal theory in the use of the term 'nullity'. It can be used to describe a pretended 'marriage' that really has no existence at all as, for example, a bigamous marriage. Or it can be used, and most commonly is, to describe a marriage that exists until either party obtains a decree of the court setting it aside, e.g. on the ground of impotence: here the annulment is no different from dissolution. A decree of nullity can also be obtained for breach of marital duty. Impotence and wilful refusal to consummate are quite different things but both are grounds for a decree of nullity.

But these illogicalities, due to the historical development of the law, are not substantial. The only substantial difference under this head between matrimonial law and common law is in relation to consent. English law has always found it difficult to draw a line between real and apparent consent where trickery is at work. The theoretical distinction—in practice often very difficult to apply in borderline cases—is between the sort of deception that empties the consent of all meaning, and the sort that induces a consent to be given which might not have been given if the truth had been known. In relation to marriage, impersonation is an example of the former and the belief that a woman is a virgin an example of the latter. In the ordinary law of contract the distinction is not of much importance as between the parties since the court can set aside a contract on either ground. In matrimonial law, deception, however grave, is not of itself a ground for relief. But there have been since 1937 two grounds for nullity that would cover express or implied deception. A marriage can be dissolved if at the time either party was suffering from a venereal disease or the woman was pregnant by another man.

Every system of law thinks it necessary to its stability that there should be some acts which once done cannot be undone. By solemnizing the performance of the act the law hopes to secure that it will not be done except with a forethought that should make revision unnecessary. No doubt in ecclesiastical law the solemnity is touched by the fact that marriage is more than the act of the parties and is a sacrament. But the common law would not have taken a different view of it. It was not until the introduction of equitable principles that the courts assumed power to set aside a formal act. There can undoubtedly be very hard cases of marriage that are induced by deception but there has not been any demand that relief should be more freely granted.

Secondly, the law prescribes the shape and obligations of the contract of marriage. In this respect it may be said that matrimonial law is radically different from the ordinary law of contract which generally leaves the parties free to make such arrangements as they like. But if the modern law reformer wanted greater freedom in this respect than the law allows (and I doubt if he does) he would have to remember that freedom of contract is now much less fashionable than it was. Since the turn of the century Parliament has in many cases dictated what the terms of a contract are to be. Landlords and tenants are now frequently joined together until the court declares the union at an end, not even death being a legal dissolvent, and the farming tenant's rights and obligations are contained in schedules lengthier and more detailed than the marriage vows.

In shaping the obligations of the contract of marriage the law operates both directly and indirectly, chiefly indirectly. Directly it operates through the rough and sparse provisions of the common law aided by equity and elaborated by the statutory jurisdiction now conferred on the Divorce Court. Indirectly it operates through what used to be the ecclesiastical law, not by translating the marriage vows into contractual clauses but by giving relief when they are broken—for adultery, desertion, cruelty, and the like. At common law the wife was the servant of the husband with no rights of her own; all her property was his. They were one in law because the wife was subordinate to and inseparable from the husband. The only duty on his part which the law had to recognize was his duty to feed, house, and clothe her. If he failed in that, she was entitled to pledge his credit for necessaries. This duty was dependent on the fulfilment by the wife of her obligations; for the woman caught in adultery there was nothing.

This conception of marriage is not now in accordance with the morality of our time. It has given way to the idea of an equal partnership between spouses, each with his or her part to play in the fulfilment of the marriage. Several influences have contributed to reshaping English law in accordance with this new morality. First, there was the influence of equity which enabled the wife to be given her separate property that could not be touched by the husband. Equitable principles were further developed in the Married Women's Property Acts. The old common law principle had been softened also by the administration of matrimonial law in the Divorce Court since it was created in 1857. Thus a husband may now be made to provide for an adulterous wife.

Equitable principles have been extended to give the wife an independent right to live in the matrimonial home; and in many modern cases the courts have striven to solve matrimonial disputes on the basis of the equal rights of the spouses. But it may be doubted if even now the wife gets her fair share of what is going. The law does not require either the husband or the wife to bring their earnings into a partnership account and as the husband is usually the breadwinner, it is the wife who suffers by this. The husband is not required to recognize in any monetary way the work that the wife does for the benefit of them both. But it is fair to say that on these points, common opinion has not yet settled and the law waits until opinion is solid. At any rate, by a series of quite remarkable developments in less than a century—remarkable when one considers the difficulty that always arises in altering judge-made law so as to keep pace with social change—the law has exorcized out of itself the old idea that the wife's personality is merged in that of the husband.

The way the law gives effect to the marriage vows is, as I have said, by giving relief for their breach. Relief for the refusal to perform the marriage act I have already considered when I spoke of nullity. Adultery, cruelty, and desertion are the three usual grounds for relief. They all represent grave breaches of the marriage vows and have always been held to do so. Desertion is plainly a suitable ground for relief, provided that it continues for a sufficiently long period to ensure that it is intended as permanent. A spouse who is deserted for such a period must be permitted to make other arrangements for his or her life. It might be said that a spouse who believed in the indissolubility of the bond should always be prepared to take back a penitent spouse, but that is to assume a degree of virtue higher than the law can reasonably require. Again, I think it would be universally agreed that the law must protect a spouse from at least the grosser forms of ill-treatment. In acknowledging that mental as well as physical cruelty can render life intolerable for the other partner, I do not think that the law has gone beyond the moral sense of the community.

In relation to adultery however, there seems to me now to have been a change of emphasis which the law has not recognized. It is the persistent association with another person, rather than the act of adultery, that breaks up the marriage; or it may be broken by repeated promiscuity. I think that in this respect there was more sense in the old law than in the new. The old law distinguished between the man's adultery and the woman's as a ground for relief. A woman could not obtain a decree of divorce for adultery unless it was coupled either with cruelty or with desertion. This was a rough and ready way of recognizing the fact that a woman does not usually commit adultery unless she intends the new association to be permanent, while a man is more casual. But in 1923 respect for the equality of the sexes induced Parliament to place the adultery of a man on the same footing as that of a woman. Many people think that, if equality was imperative, society would have been better served by the restriction of the male rather than by the liberation of the female.

These are criticisms of the detail of the law, and, if they are valid, amending legislation can give effect to them without altering the fundamental structure. Fundamentally, I do not think that there is much dissatisfaction with the law in its operation as between husband and wife and in its formulation of the ground for relief, if relief be confined to judicial separation. It is true that when a marriage goes wrong, there are generally faults on both sides; and it can be said that there is something artificial in trying to categorize the breaches of obligation and squeeze them into the three categories I have named. But if one party is demanding a judicial separation which the other opposes, it is necessary for the petitioner to show some grave fault and it is difficult to see how the law can be less precise. In practice separation is rarely opposed. No spouse, whether he or she is at fault or not, wants to continue conjugal relations with another person who is unwilling to give them freely. The controversy occurs over the provision that is to be made, as a result of the separation, financially or for the care and custody of the children. In such a controversy our law does not now regard the commission of matrimonial offences as the only relevant factor though, as I think is right, they are bound to play some part in the decision. Where custody is in dispute the welfare of the child is the paramount consideration and it is frequently given to the guilty party. When alimony or maintenance is being fixed, guilt or innocence must be the starting-point. But no one now supposes that an adulterous wife ought inevitably to be left without means of support.

Thus, although English matrimonial law is a mixture of overlapping jurisdictions and ideas and there is nothing neat or tidy about it, it does, I think, give effect fairly satisfactorily to what are now recognized as being the moral obligations of the spouses towards each other. The rights and obligations between the spouses on the one hand and third parties on the other is still confused by the notion that husband and wife are one in law. As I have said, the spouses cannot be treated in their relations with third parties as if they were two disunited individuals. English law deals with this sort of problem in one of two ways: it starts either from reality or from fiction. When it starts from reality, as in the case of a firm or partnership or of principal and agent, it treats the individuals as separate entities, which they are, and makes special provision for the peculiar nature of their relationship. Otherwise, it creates a single legal entity, as in the case of a limited company, to personify the union. In marriage it has begun by following the latter course by means of the fiction that husband and wife are one in law. This fiction is gradually yielding to statutory treatment and further reform is a matter of modernization rather than of morals. But it is still preserved in one unhappy respect which I shall elaborate when I come to consider the third category.

I have finished now with the rights and obligations that flow from marriage both as between the parties themselves and towards those with whom as partners in marriage they have to deal. I pass on to what I have suggested should properly be regarded as a quite distinct branch of the law and what therefore I have separated into a second category, that is, the conditions under which the State should licence or permit marriages, first, second, or third. About the licensing of first marriages or of second marriages of widows or widowers there is no issue to speak of. The permitting of any other sort of second marriage is, I have said, in substance the same thing as the grant of a divorce of the first. The two things are however very different in form. Does the form matter? If you agree with me, you will accept that the only temporal difference between divorce and judicial separation is that in the former case the parties can marry again and in the latter they cannot. You may accept that the main, if not the only, reason why a petitioner seeks a divorce rather than a judicial separation is because he feels that sooner or later he may want to marry again. You may agree that the logical way of achieving that would be to have two separate and distinct processes—one for a judicial separation and the second for another marriage licence. By the first process the parties are released from one set of temporal obligations towards a specific person; and by the second they are permitted to enter into a similar set of obligations towards another person. But if in an old-fashioned way the State chooses to do it by saying that the first marriage—whatever the parties may think about it and whatever their religion may require their consciences to think—for the purposes of the law remains spiritually alive until it is dissolved by the court and that while it is alive the parties may not enter into another one, does it not achieve the same thing?

I think that the result is the same. But the process leading to the result is or should be entirely different. Because the application to marry again is granted in the form of a divorce decree, it is regarded as a form of relief *inter partes*. You may call the grant of freedom to remarry a 'relief' if you like, but it has nothing to do with the *lis* between the parties. When the court has discharged the petitioner from his material obligations, the *lis* is over and done with. Up till then the *lis* has been a private affair and the State has not been able to intervene because it cannot enforce conjugal rights on unwilling spouses and has long since given up the attempt to do so. But on an application by the petitioner for leave to marry again the State can do more than intervene; it can claim that such an application is the concern of the State and of the State alone and that the respondent has no right to be heard on it. They are two entirely different processes—the first private and the second public. It is wrong to treat the second process as if it were only the natural sequel to or fulfilment of the first.

The confusion between the private and the public process has led inevitably to two errors. The first is that an innocent petitioner is allowed as of right to marry again. Since the only thing that ought to be considered is the public interest, the fact that the respondent has committed a matrimonial offence ought not to be conclusive. I do not mean that the petitioner's innocence is irrelevant—far from it. Nor by using the term 'public interest' do I mean to convey the idea that the matter is to be decided purely by the application of general principles and without regard to the particular circumstances and the happiness and welfare of the individuals concerned. These matters *are* matters of public interest. The factors to be considered are of the same nature as those which are considered by the court in cases where it has a discretion to grant or withhold the decree, that is, under the present law, where both parties are guilty of matrimonial offences. The interests of the children come first. Then there have to be considered the interests of the parties themselves and of any third person who might be involved in a new marriage and the interests of the community generally. If there is added to these the innocence of the injured spouse as a factor to be given great weight, it is probable that in the present climate of opinion at any rate that factor would rarely be outweighed. But it remains true as a matter of principle that what is or is not in the public interest cannot be settled in advance by the application of a rule of thumb. If it had never been supposed that it could, the present climate of opinion might not be as lax as it now is.

The second error is of the same sort as the one I have just considered but it has been much more catastrophic in its results. If the public process had been regarded as an application for a licence to marry again, it could never have been supposed that it ought automatically to be granted, not merely to the injured party but also to the offender. It was supposed that this result must necessarily follow from the dissolution of the spiritual bond; it could not be untied in such a way as to leave one party bound. That may be sound logic but the logic depends on the assertion that the State is concerned with the spiritual bond.

When guilty behaviour leads to desirable results, there will be people who will not mind behaving guiltily in order to secure those results. They will give grounds for divorce. The cardinal error in the development of the law was to ignore this obvious fact, so that the legal system has never been equipped with adequate machinery for dealing with it. The British legal system is based on the assumption that the truth, so far as it is necessary for the court to know it in order to do justice, will emerge from the conflict between two opponents. The judge is not an inquisitor with instruments at his own disposal for ascertainment of the facts. No fact is brought before him unless it is in the interests of one side or the other to prove it. The assumption is that he will get all the relevant facts in that way and that he will adjudicate upon them as an arbiter. The system works normally in divorce procedure up to the point of the judicial separation. No one is likely to admit guilt unless it is to his interests to do so and no one is likely to have an interest in obtaining a judicial separation by an order of the court rather than by consent. The system would work well enough also if the public process had been distinguished from the private. Then in the petition for divorce the State would be the respondent. Instead of this, the process is treated as one and indivisible and the public interest is treated as incidental and as sufficiently safeguarded by the rule that the judge must be satisfied on the petitioner's evidence that he has proved his case and must not be satisfied that he has done so with the collusive aid of the other side. It is only if an irregularity accidentally emerges that the State intervenes through the Queen's Proctor. It is notorious that these safeguards have proved worthless. It is as silly as if two insured motorists were left to litigate between each other about the responsibility for a road accident and the result held to be binding on their insurance companies. The funds of the companies could not suffer more, if that were the common law, than public morality has suffered by the operation of the divorce laws.

All this, the free-thinker asserts, is the result of having a State religion in which no citizen is compelled to believe. If belief were compulsory, there would be no remarriage except where the church permitted it. If the Church of England were not the established church, it would never have occurred to anyone that the functions of the ecclesiastical courts could by a stroke of the pen be transferred to the secular courts. Thus the criticism of our divorce law is not so much that it is out of touch with common morality as that it does not provide the means by which the moral sense of the community can be made effective. The fault goes right back to 1857. The mistake then was that the decree of divorce was brought in as if it were only an additional form of relief whose introduction required no substantial alteration to the structure of the law. So long as respectability operated as a motive force on the individual, the nature of this defect was concealed. The interest of a respondent charged with a matrimonial offence which it was disreputable to admit, coincided with the public interest and so both worked against easy divorce. When the status of a divorced person ceased to be a social disability, the machinery of the law began to break down. What keeps it functioning now to a limited extent is a similar force of self-interest. There is reluctance to admit a matrimonial offence if it is likely to affect orders for custody or maintenance which cannot be agreed. But this is not a factor which seems substantially to diminish the number of divorces by consent.

There is something unreal about discussing grounds of divorce and debating whether they should be narrowed or widened. It is like designing products for manufacture by a machine that is so antiquated that it has almost ceased to work. If the grounds are widened, the process is easier to fake; if they are narrowed it is more difficult. That is really all that reform of the law since 1857 has accomplished. The sacred principle is preserved. All who desire their freedom from the bond must pass out of the hall of judgement. At the main gateway there stand custodians and there is exhibited a schedule of conditions under which permission is granted to leave. But the back door is unlocked and unguarded. Every now and again someone is caught sneaking out and is at once hustled in again with cries of disapproval. What is the use of discussing amendments to the schedule so long as the back door is left unbolted? There is some value in it certainly. It affects the lot of those who have a distaste for using back doors, but that is all.

I think that any satisfactory reform of the law would have to be based upon a distinction between the private and the public process and that the latter had best be built upon entirely new foundations. But most of us dislike changes of form and the British public would not take kindly to the idea of regulation by marriage licence. The existing law could, I think, be adapted to work under four conditions. Firstly, the public must be properly represented. Since a petition for divorce is really a petition to be allowed to remarry, the State is the real respondent. Secondly, the decree must operate only in favour of the party who asks for it, whether he be petitioner or respondent in the proceedings *inter partes*. Thirdly, the granting of it must always be discretionary. Fourthly, the discretion must be unfettered. There is no room in the public process, as distinct from the private, for 'grounds for divorce'. The object of the public inquiry is to find out whether the public interest would be injured by a fresh marriage. Is there sincerity? That is the question, if it can be put into a word. The justification of the new marriage is the breakdown of the old despite sincere attempts to make it work. It is only in its bearing upon that that the matrimonial offence is significant. The public interest also requires that proper provision should be made for the wife and children of the first marriage, for if a man has not the will or the means to support two households there is a lack of responsibility that bodes ill for the second marriage. The public interest would not comprehend a veto on remarriage by the other spouse such as can be effective today.

I suppose that in the present climate of opinion a decree of divorce would rarely be refused. It might have been different if divorce had always been discretionary, but we have lived too long with a legal system incapable of preventing divorce by consent. But I believe that even now the moral sense of the community would support the refusal of a decree when it appeared to the court that marriage was being treated as no more than a licensed *affaire*.

These ideas, although they involve a different approach to the problem, do not mean that in the majority of cases the court would be at work in an unfamiliar field. A judge is very used to trying to discern where the public interest lies and his task will be aided and not altered in that by a proper elucidation of the facts. The requirements of cruelty, physical or mental, and desertion, actual or constructive, are often now no more than formulae for testing whether the marriage has genuinely broken down. There are also so many cases now in which both parties are at fault that the decree is often discretionary.

I have now made my point about the true effect of a decree of divorce, that in reality it is only the means whereby the State permits a second marriage; and I have suggested how within the present formal framework the law might be altered so that the principles on which it is administered correspond more closely with reality. In so doing I have assumed that the State has the moral right to refuse permission for a second marriage. I must now consider the validity of that assumption.

The interest of the State in marriage comes from two different sources. The first is general: it has an interest in monogamy as an institution. The second is particular: it has an interest in the welfare of any children of the marriage. Both these interests are generally admitted. No one suggests that bigamy should be permitted or that the State should not regulate the terms of marriage. The question is whether in a society which insists on monogamy based on a free and voluntary contract between two individuals, the State can deny the right of free and voluntary dissolution so as to prevent the parties from contracting again. It is as well, I think, to get out of the way at once the particular interest of the State. There are not many people who would deny on moral grounds the right of the State to control dissolution where there are children of the marriage. Some would say that any attempt at control is futile and that the lot of the children cannot be improved by forbidding remarriage to parents who will not live together. Others would say that the best preservative of family life is to make it clear that parents with responsibilities to children have no hope at all of divorce. But these are sociological and not moral arguments. The effective way of testing the morality of State interference is in relation to the childless marriage.

I have spoken of State interference. That is the way in which those who say that the childless marriage is no concern of society are apt to think of it. But is it the right way? There is here no question of oppression. In a free society the State is not thought to be at liberty to prohibit a practice merely because the vast majority of citizens dislike it. It should not, for example, to take a subject of current controversy in relation to the enforcement of morals, prohibit association between homosexual adults unless the notion offends so deeply the morality of the society in which they live that it is not to be tolerated at all. But that is not the test to be applied here. The law does not prohibit sexual unions outside marriage. Marriage, when stripped of its spiritual significance, is simply a special sort of union between a man and a woman to which society gives a special status. No individual can claim to be oppressed because society will not give him that status on his own terms. The complaint of the man who wants to be free to dissolve his marriage whenever his partner consents is not that he cannot take another partner when he chooses and live with her, but that he cannot do so with the approval of society.

Is then the State according to our ideas of society entirely free to grant or withhold the status of marriage as it is, for example, free to confer or not the status of the peerage? No. A man and a woman who live together outside marriage are not prosecuted under the law but they are not protected by it. They are outside the law. Their union is not recognized, no legal obligation is implicit in it, and an express obligation will not be enforced by the law. Prima facie the individual is entitled to call upon the law to enforce the contracts which he makes. That is a service which should be performed by the law of contract. Freedom of contract requires that the law should in general recognize and enforce whatever contracts are voluntarily entered into unless they are anti-social. English law has from the earliest times refused to enforce certain classes of contracts as being against public policy. Irregular sexual unions constitute one of those classes. Statutes have recently added enormously to the area in which freedom of contract is restricted and the freedom óf the individual is not now thought to require that all legislation of this sort should be condemned. It is enough that the restraint should not be imposed unless it serves some important social purpose. The decision whether it does or not is a political and not a moral one. That means that in a democracy it must, broadly speaking, accord with the will of the majority. Society has a right therefore to define the status of marriage in accordance with the ideas of the majority and to refuse to confer it upon those who do not conform.

A society which permits no divorce at all may still properly regard itself as a free society. If the general feeling in that society, whether it springs from a religious source or from any other, is that marriage is something which ought to be dissolved only by death, then that is the sort of marriage that that society is entitled to have. I do not think that in Britain today there is a general feeling of this sort. I do not say that simply because divorce is legal. It quite often happens that the moral law disapproves of something which the secular law permits as a concession to human frailty.

But it is also possible to take the view that an unqualified insistence upon the indissolubility of marriage is morally wrong; that there is no moral justification for denying to a person, whose religious beliefs do not sustain the denial, the fulfilment of a happy marriage; that no good social purpose is served by outlawing a sincere union of that sort. I believe that that is the morality which, outside religion, prevails in Britain today. British morality wants a compromise between two extremes of the sort that was recognized and expressed by Lord Chancellor Simon in 1943. In describing 'the interest of the community at large' as one of the most important factors to be borne in mind by the court where it had a discretion to grant or refuse a decree he said that it was to be judged 'by maintaining a true balance between respect for the binding sanctity of marriage and the social considerations which make it contrary to public policy to insist on the maintenance of a union which has utterly broken down'.[1] I believe that our morality still dislikes the idea of marriage not being taken very seriously. It expects the

[1] *Blunt* v. *Blunt* (1943) A.C. 517 at 525.

parties to intend a lifelong union and to be willing to sacrifice much to the fulfilment of that intention, but it thinks that spouses who have done their best and failed should be allowed to try again. If that be our idea of marriage I do not see why it should not afford a sound moral basis for our law.

I suppose that in theory the State might refuse to license even a first marriage if it were dissatisfied about the sincerity of the parties and certainly there are some people whose morals make them wholly unfit for marriage. Yet marriage is so much a part of the natural order that in most societies it would be thought intolerable if any restrictions of this sort were placed upon it in the first instance. But I do not see why society should not, when a marriage has failed, claim the right to demand proofs of sincerity before it licenses another. If to a particular society monogamy means no more than only living with one person at one time, there is no point in restricting divorce; but if to any particular society it means more than that, society must have the right of refusing the status.

I hope that I have now satisfied the free-thinker that the State has a right on moral grounds—not merely on religious; he rightly objects to their introduction—to regulate remarriage. The refusal to permit divorce by consent can be justified quite apart from religion as is shown by legislation in the U.S.S.R. Originally, after the Revolution of 1917, divorce by consent was permitted and no reason had to be given; the court could not refuse a decree. Since 1944 it has been discretionary and in an Order made in 1949 the Supreme Court of the U.S.S.R. said that it should be granted only where there were 'deeply considered and well-founded reasons' and where 'continuation of the marriage would conflict with the principles of communist morals and could not create the conditions necessary to family law and the rearing of children'.[1]

I may also have satisfied the free-thinker to a large extent with my acceptance of the need for radical reform in the existing law. Why then, he asks, should we not clean up the law on these lines? It is not as if, he says with truth, he wants to throw marriage on the scrap heap or make divorce any easier than it is now in practice. What he wants is to secure that divorce or freedom to remarry is available to all on grounds that are acceptable to decent members of the community and not just on any ground to colluders and deceivers.

[1] See Friedmann's *Law in a Changing Society*, 1951, p. 212.

The only reason, he feels, why reform is opposed is because those who believe in the indissolubility of marriage want to enforce their belief on others; they are fighting for theology and not for morals.

There is a great deal of truth in this. I think that the opposition to radical reform does consist largely of men with religious beliefs who accept the biblical conception of marriage. What I have outlined as a measure of radical reform is a blue-print for a society that treats religious belief purely as a matter of conscience and does not accept faith as a factor that should condition the law. There is no place in the blue-print for marriage as a sacrament. It presupposes that men and women make and unmake their own marriages and that the State is only the registrar, albeit one invested with some power to disallow. The merit of the existing law in the eyes of those who support it—indeed the essence of it which must at all costs be retained—is that it accepts marriage as a bond which the parties themselves cannot loosen but which can be dissolved only by a higher authority. That is the sacred principle. I used those words earlier in this lecture and neither then nor now did I mean them with a sneer.

Men who believe in the sacred principle do not blind themselves to the fact that the cause shown for divorce is often faked or illusory. But abuse of the law does not justify the abandonment of the principle behind the law. The essence of that principle is that there is a marriage bond that can be broken by misconduct but cannot otherwise be dissolved by the act of either party. One clear testing point of the difference between the two views is in their attitude towards the spouse who will not divorce the partner who wants it and has given grounds for it. To some people this seems morally and socially indefensible. If it is, in the words of Lord Simon, 'contrary to public policy to insist on the maintenance of a union which has utterly broken down', how can it be right to place that power in the hands of a single individual with a grievance? But if marriage is a spiritual bond, how can it be right to dissolve it against the will of an innocent spouse?

I have now, the free-thinker would say, let the cat out of the bag. The whole question is whether or not marriage is to be treated as a contract which, when duly solemnized, has spiritual as well as temporal force. If it is to be recognized by the law of the land as having spiritual force, then plainly it must continue until the divorce court, claiming some sort of spiritual inheritance from the ecclesiastical court and administering some sort of theology diluted by practical considerations, declares it to be at an end. If on the other hand it has only temporal force derived solely from mutual consent, there is no power on earth that can keep it alive after the parties themselves have extinguished it.

I think it is completely true to say that the opposition to the wholesale reform of the divorce law which logic demands is based on, and can only be justified by, the belief that marriage creates a sacramental bond. That takes me back to the assumption with which I began this lecture that it is not permissible in a secular society to justify any law by assuming a religious belief. Does this close the argument?

I think not entirely. There is yet something more to be said on that. But before I say it let me deal with the third object which I assigned to the law, for it brings out a point that will illustrate what I want to say further. The law should seek, I suggested, to favour marriage in the same way as it fosters any other institution that is good for society. This, as I said, is primarily a matter of sociology. It is accepted as part of the function of the modern State that it should assist or discourage activities and institutions of which it approves or disapproves. What does it do to encourage marriage? The answer is nothing. It does a great deal for the family but it does not very much mind whether or not the family is legitimate. This is perhaps inevitable. Children cannot because of the fault of their parents be deprived of advantages they would otherwise have had. There would be something wrong with a society, it might be said, in which the State had to subsidize virtue.

But equally, it may be said, there is something wrong with a State which *penalizes* virtue. That is what is now being done in Britain on a large scale; and since that is made possible only through the operation of an old common law principle, it is a phenomenon which deserves attention in a lecture of this sort. I have said that the process was now almost complete by which the law has exorcized out of itself the bad old notion that the wife was not to be treated as an individual human being but only as an extension of her husband's legal personality. There is however one branch of the law in which the old notion is still held in great reverence and that is the law of income tax.

When this tax was originated in Britain the wife could have had no separate income so that there could have been no question of taxing her as an individual. The idea of marriage as a partnership changes that. If the law had lumped all the income of business partners together for the purposes of surtax, there would by now be no firms left; everyone would trade singly or in a company. When death duties were introduced in 1894, there was no difficulty felt about treating the wife as a separate individual so as to tax her on the capital left for her widowhood. It often happens however, in the law of England, that a principle of law, notwithstanding that its original ratio has gone, is preserved because of its serviceability in unintended ways. Three grounds of justification are commonly advanced for the present law of taxation of husband and wife.

The first and weakest is that since they share a joint household, which is cheaper than two separate ones, they should be jointly taxed. This applies also to two business partners who share their office, to a brother and sister who share a dwelling place, to a lover and his mistress, and to two homosexuals who live together, but none of these couples is jointly taxed. What savings they make by means of a joint *ménage* they can spend as they like, while in the case of husband and wife the savings are often far outweighed by the expenses of a family.

Then it is said that the wife's earned income allowance (introduced not for the purpose of assisting marriage but in order to entice female labour into the factories) puts the matter right for the most deserving part of the community—a part which is taken to exclude everyone with an earned income above the average or with any income from property. I have two things to say about that. The allowance seems to me from the social point of view to be an undesirable expedient. Few women nowadays are idle and the effect of the allowance is to benefit those who work outside the home and the family instead of within it. It may be desirable economically to attract women into industry but it is not a good thing socially or morally when a similar allowance is withheld from those who work in the home. The second thing is that the moral tone of a community is set more by the upper than by the lower half; change works downwards and not upwards. The fact is that for a large part of the community, mainly but not altogether in the upper half, marriage is taxed and liaisons are free. So are former wives. In a few cases this can amount almost to a scandal. What a man gives to his wedded wife comes entirely out of his own pocket. Much of what he pays to a former wife by way of alimony or maintenance he would otherwise pay to the Exchequer. A very rich man could keep half a dozen former wives for the price of one in wedlock; and that does nothing to discourage divorce.

Thirdly it is said that any change is impracticable because the loss of revenue could not be made good. This is the last and always the most formidable of all the ditches that are dug around every fortress of injustice. In fact the change has been found quite practicable in several countries with a social and economic background similar to ours; I have in mind the United States, Australia, and Canada. But I am concerned here not so much with economics as with the effect on the nation's morals. It is no good treating marriage as if it were a bad habit like smoking or drinking which it would be financially distressing but morally improving to tax out of existence. A nation that is raising revenue out of marriage is selling morals for cash and must not be surprised if its stock of morals dwindles. So far the market has held out. But as all speculators know, a market which looks as if it was going on for ever making money for everybody with no one being able to see why it should ever come to an end, can suddenly collapse. One day a couple with no religious beliefs will make a public announcement that they propose to live together as man and wife but that for reasons of taxation they are not going through a form of marriage. Then contagion will spread and a government that is faced with a loss of money as well as of morals will act to save the former and find the latter to be beyond salvage.

What I have been saying is a very forcible reminder of the extent to which the government of a State rests upon the moral virtue of its subjects. The law cannot make people good; it can only punish them for being bad or at least discourage them. The State must rely on other agencies besides the law, and that brings me to my concluding theme. The sociologist and the man of faith both believe in the value of marriage, the latter because it is ordained by God-and spiritually good and the former because it is an institution necessary to the society in which he lives. Both therefore want to see that it continues to be popularly observed and to encourage the forces behind it. The main force that lies behind the observance of the marriage vows for the ordinary man is religion or a teaching that is embedded in him, having been derived from religion. It is not too much to say that religion is necessary to the institution of marriage.

In law-making logic will always be defeated by necessity. The weakness of the free-thinker's position is that he offers no substitute for religion as a social force. There was a time at the beginning of this century when it was thought that the goal of a perfect society would be attractive enough. The denial that the profit motive was necessary is one example. Men did not need it, it was said. Remove the capitalists and all would be well: so soon as labourers realized that they were working not to make fuller the purses of the rich but for the good of all, there would be industrial peace. Likewise, it was said that so soon as the wicked despots who controlled the affairs of nations for their own ends were driven from their thrones, the people would rise up and fall into each other's arms in brotherly love. All this events have falsified. It still needs the divine promise to divert the mass of mankind to higher things. Thousands of men and women who are not church-goers persevere with the obligations of marriage and resist temptation because marriage means more to them than an institution of high social value. Morality and religion are so inextricably intertwined in the mind of the ordinary man that the wise sociologist has to accept that they cannot just be wrenched apart. There are individuals who can lead perfect lives by charity alone but for men and women as a whole, and so for society, there must also be faith and hope. A man can make his own philosophy. To make a philosophy for a society is far more difficult; and so far in the western world only Christianity has succeeded. The question for the social reformer is not whether Christianity is right or wrong but whether it is dispensable. If he has his feet on the ground, he knows that it is not. The appeal to logic is not the end. He would be foolish to attempt to drive through a radical reform against the opposition of the churches.

Nevertheless I think the signs are that opposition is being undermined. I do not mean that the attitude of the churches towards divorce is weakening; all the signs there are to the contrary. But I think that churchmen are from one point of view becoming just as dissatisfied with the coalition between the law and religion as are free-thinkers from the other. Whatever the theory may be, the Church of England does not in practice recognize the decree of divorce as a dissolution of the sacramental bond and it can now only be embarrassed by the thought that things of the spirit are being regulated from the Strand.

The idea that marriage and divorce should be dealt with by the law as if they were matters without religious significance is, I know, distressing to many good people. But to my mind the time has come for a clean break and both the church and the law would be stronger for it. The mingling of the spiritual and the temporal jurisdictions has been good for neither. The break-up of the coalition need not destroy an alliance in which both parties, following different principles, are working for the same end, the moral good of the community. It is in this way, it is now recognized, rather than by the assimilation of doctrine, that the divisions within Christendom can best be remedied. The law, which knows nothing of such divisions, should know nothing either of the gap that divides the good Christian from the good agnostic. It must be wide enough to express the moral ideals of both.

Just as the wise free-thinker must acknowledge that the support of Christianity is of the utmost value to the law, so the wise Christian must acknowledge that the support of the law is of high value to Christianity. What allies the two are the objects which they have in common. It would be tragic if those objects were frustrated because Christians insisted upon the embodiment of doctrine in the marriage law and despised the law for its weakness if it did not comply; or if free-thinkers treated the support which Christianity gives to the institution of marriage with nothing but a *non tali auxilio*.[1] The State needs the goodwill of both. I would not deny that the breadth of the moral law in a free-thinking community saps its strength in particular sectors of the line. But that is the price we must pay for freedom of conscience.

---

[1] *non tali auxilio nec defensoribus istis . . .*, Virgil, *Aeneid*, II, 521: 'not [with] such assistance or defenders such as those . . .'.

V

Democracy and Morality*

When a state recognizes freedom of worship and of conscience, it sets a problem for jurists which they have not yet succeeded in solving. Now, when the law divides right from wrong, it cannot appeal to any absolute authority outside itself as justifying the division. All the questions which before were settled by divine law as pronounced by the churches are thrown open to debate when the decision is taken to admit freedom of conscience.

This decision, and not the separation of Church from State, is crucial. In England, the Church has never been formally separated from the State, but by the beginning of the nineteenth century an Englishman was effectively set free to worship or not as he chose. It was freedom not to worship at all and to disbelieve in revelation that was important, for it deprived the law of spiritual sustenance. In the eyes of the law the only judgement upon right and wrong which a man could be expected to follow was that of his own conscience, and it did not matter whether he taught himself on matters of morals or was taught by others.

The nineteenth-century English philosophers drew what appeared to be the logical conclusion from the change. While the political scientists and constitution-makers of the age were engaged in separating Church and State, the philosophers came near to separating law and morality. Austin taught that the only force behind the law was physical force. Mill declared that the only purpose for which that force could rightfully be used against any member of the community was to prevent harm to others; his own good, physical or moral, was not sufficient warrant.

But this sort of thinking made no impact at all upon the development or administration of the English criminal law. This was doubtless because no practical problems arose. If there had been a

* The Owen J. Roberts Memorial Lecture, delivered 28 September 1961, under the auspices of the Pennsylvania Chapter of the Order of the Coif and the University of Pennsylvania Law School, and printed in the *University of Pennsylvania Law Review*, vol. 110, p. 635.

deep division in the country on matters of morals—if there had been, for example, a large minority who wished to practise polygamy—the theoretical basis for legislation on morals would have had to have been scrutinized. But the Englishman's hundred religions about which Voltaire made his jibe gave rise to no differences on morals grave enough to affect the criminal law. Parliament added incest and homosexual offences to the list of crimes without inquiring what harm they did to the community if they were committed in private; it was enough that they were morally wrong. The judges continued to administer the law on the footing that England was a Christian country. Reluctantly they recognized respectful criticism of Christian doctrine as permissible and the crime of blasphemy virtually disappeared. But Christian morals remained embedded in the law.[1]

It is only recently that there has emerged a moral problem needing a practical solution. There have often been cases in which men have violated various precepts of moral law, but there has been no body of men who asserted that the law ought not to interfere with immoral behaviour. There are now in England men who secretly see nothing wrong with the homosexual relationship. There are others, to be found mainly among the educated classes, who, while not themselves practising homosexuality, are not repelled by it, think it a permissible way of life for those so constituted as to enjoy it, and deplore the misery the law inflicts on the comparatively few victims it detects. In September 1957 the Wolfenden Committee of thirteen distinguished men and women appointed by the Home Secretary recommended with only one dissenter that homosexual behaviour between consenting adults in private should no longer be a criminal offence; and they based their recommendation on the ground that such offences were 'not the law's business'.[2] The Home Secretary did not accept this recommendation; nevertheless, the report, in addition to its sociological value, is an important statement on the relationship between the criminal and the moral law.

Another landmark was made in May 1961 by the decision of the House of Lords in *Shaw* v. *Director of Public Prosecutions*.[3] This case

---

[1] The change is described by Lord Radcliffe in his 1960 Rosenthal Lectures, *Law and Its Compass*. Mr. Justice Phillimore put the point broadly when he said: 'A man is free to think, to speak and to teach what he pleases as to religious matters, though not as to morals.' *Rex* v. *Boulter* (1908), 72 J.P. 188.

[2] Wolfenden, para. 61. [3] (1962) A.C. 220.

arose indirectly out of another recommendation by the Wolfenden Committee. They were asked to report also upon offences in connection with prostitution; and as a result the Street Offences Act, 1959,[1] which stopped prostitutes soliciting in the streets, was passed. Mr. Shaw naïvely considered that since Parliament had not prohibited the trade of prostitution, there could be nothing objectionable or illegal about his supplying for prostitutes some means of advertisement in place of that which Parliament had denied them. So he published a magazine, which he called 'The Ladies' Directory', containing the names, addresses, and telephone numbers of prostitutes. If that were all that he had done and if he had been content to remunerate himself simply by the proceeds from the sale of the magazine, he would have committed no specific offence. But the magazine contained additional matter which made it an obscene libel; and by taking payment from the prostitutes themselves the defendant had committed the statutory offence of living 'wholly or in part on the earnings of prostitution'.[2] The importance of the case comes from the first count in the indictment, which was independent of the two statutory offences and alleged a conspiracy at common law to corrupt public morals, the particulars being that the defendant and the prostitutes who advertised themselves in his magazine conspired 'to induce readers thereof to resort to the said advertisers for the purposes of fornication'.[3] The defence argued that there was no such general offence known to the law as a conspiracy to corrupt public morals, but the House of Lords held by a majority of four to one that there was and that the accused was rightly found guilty of it. Viscount Simonds said: 'There remains in the courts of law a residual power to enforce the supreme and fundamental purpose of the law, to conserve not only the safety and order but also the moral welfare of the State';[4] and he approved the assertion of Lord Mansfield two centuries before that the Court of King's Bench was the *custos morum* of the people and had the superintendency of offences *contra bonos mores*.[5]

With this cardinal enunciation of principle the courts rejected the teaching of John Stuart Mill and proclaimed themselves keepers of

---

[1] 7 & 8 Eliz. 2, c. 57.

[2] Sexual Offences Act, 1956, 4 & 5 Eliz. 2, c. 69, s. 30(1).

[3] The particulars also specified an invitation to indulge in certain perversions. The House of Lords did not treat this as making much—if any—difference.

[4] *Shaw* v. *Director of Public Prosecutions, supra,* at 267.

[5] *Rex* v. *Delaval* (1763) 3 Burr. 1434 at 1438; 97 E.R. 913 at 915.

the nation's morals. From what source do they draw that power and how do they ascertain the moral standards they enforce?

The State may claim on two grounds to legislate on matters of morals. The Platonic ideal is that the State exists to promote virtue among its citizens. If that is its function, then whatever power is sovereign in the State—an autocrat, if there be one, or in a democracy the majority—must have the right and duty to declare what standards of morality are to be observed as virtuous and must ascertain them as it thinks best. This is not acceptable to Anglo-American thought. It invests the State with power of determination between good and evil, destroys freedom of conscience and is the paved road to tyranny. It is against this concept of the State's power that Mill's words are chiefly directed.

The alternative ground is that society may legislate to preserve itself. This is the ground, I think, taken by Lord Simonds when he says that the purpose of the law is to conserve the moral welfare of the State; and all the speeches in the House show, especially when they are laying down the part to be played by the jury, that the work of the courts is to be the guarding of a heritage and not the creation of a system. 'The ultimate foundation of a free society is the binding tie of cohesive sentiment.'[1] What makes a society is a community of ideas, not political ideas alone but also ideas about the way its members should behave and govern their lives.

A law that enforces moral standards must, like any other law, be enacted by the appropriate constitutional organ, the monarch or the legislative majority as the case may be. The essential difference between the two theories is that under the first the law-maker must determine for himself what is good for his subjects. He may be expected to do so not arbitrarily but to the best of his understanding; but it is his decision, based on his judgement of what is best, from which alone the law derives authority. The democratic system of government goes some way—not all the way, for no representative can be the mirror of the voters' thoughts—to ensure that the decision of the law-maker will be acceptable to the majority, but the majority is not the whole. A written constitution may safeguard to a great extent and for a long time the conscience of a minority, but not entirely and forever; for a written constitution is only a fundamental enactment that is difficult to alter.

But under the second theory the law-maker is not required to

[1] *Minersville School Dist.* v. *Gobitis*, 310 U.S. 586, 596 (1940) (Frankfurter, J.).

make any judgement about what is good and what is bad. The morals which he enforces are those ideas about right and wrong which are already accepted by the society for which he is legislating and which are necessary to preserve its integrity. He has not to argue with himself about the merits of monogamy and polygamy; he has merely to observe that monogamy is an essential part of the structure of the society to which he belongs. Naturally he will assume that the morals of his society are good and true; if he does not, he should not be playing an active part in government. But he has not to vouch for their goodness and truth. His mandate is to preserve the essentials of his society, not to reconstruct them according to his own ideas.

How does the law-maker ascertain the moral principles that are accepted by the society to which he belongs? He is concerned only with the fundament that is surely accepted, for legal sanctions are inappropriate for the enforcement of moral standards that are in dispute. He does not therefore need the assistance of moral philosophers nor does he have to study the arguments upon peripheral questions. He is concerned with what is acceptable to the ordinary man, the man in the jury box, who might also be called the reasonable man or the rightminded man. When I call him the man in the jury box, I do not mean to imply that the ordinary citizen when he enters the jury box is invested with some peculiar quality that enables him to pronounce *ex cathedra* on morals. I still think of him simply as the ordinary reasonable man, but by placing him in the jury box I call attention to three points. First, the verdict of a jury must be unanimous; so a moral principle, if it is to be given the force of law, should be one which twelve men and women drawn at random from the community can be expected not only to approve but to take so seriously that they regard a breach of it as fit for punishment. Second, the man in the jury box does not give a snap judgement but returns his verdict after argument, instruction, and deliberation. Third, the jury box is a place in which the ordinary man's views on morals become directly effective. The law-maker who makes the mistake of thinking that what he has to preserve is not the health of society but a particular regimen, will find that particular laws wither away. An important part of the machinery for hastening obsolescence is the lay element in the administration of English justice, the man in the jury box and the lay magistrate. The magistrates can act by the imposition of nominal penalties; the juryman acts by acquittal. If he gravely dislikes a law or thinks its application too harsh, he has the power, which from time immemorial he has exercised, to return a verdict of acquittal that is unassailable; and of its unassailability in English law William Penn and Bushell the juror stand as immortal witnesses.[1]

This gives the common man, when sitting in the jury box, a sort of veto upon the enforcement of morals. One of the most interesting features of *Shaw*'s case is that (in cases of uncategorized immorality contrary to common law as distinct from offences defined by statute) it confers on the jury a right and duty more potent than an unofficial veto; it makes the jury a constitutional organ for determining what amounts to immorality and when the law should be enforced. I shall return to that later.

What I want to discuss immediately is the reaction that many philosophers and academic lawyers have to the doctrine I have just outlined. They dislike it very much. It reduces morality, they feel, to the level of a question of fact. What Professor H. L. A. Hart calls rationalist morality,[2] which I take to be morality embodied in the rational judgement of men who have studied moral questions and pondered long on what the answers ought to be, will be blown aside by a gust of popular morality compounded of all the irrational prejudices and emotions of the man in the street. Societies in the past have tolerated witch-hunting and burnt heretics: was that done in the name of morality? There are societies today whose moral standards permit them to discriminate against men because of their colour: have we to accept that? Is reason to play no part in the separation of right from wrong?

The most significant thing about questions of this type is that none of the questioners would think them worth asking if the point at issue had nothing in it of the spiritual. It is a commonplace that in our sort of society matters of great moment are settled in accordance with the opinion of the ordinary citizen who acts no more and no less rationally in matters of policy than in matters of morals. Such is the consequence of democracy and universal suffrage. Those who have had the benefit of a higher education and feel themselves better equipped to solve the nation's problems than the average may find

---

[1] See *Bushell*'s Case (1670), Jones 1, at 13, 84 Eng. Rep. 1123.

[2] Hart, 'Immorality and Treason', *The Listener*, 1959, vol. 62, pp. 162, 163. Professor Hart's views on this point have been considered by Dean Rostow in 'The Enforcement of Morals', *Cambridge Law Journal*, 1960, pp. 174, 184–92. I cannot improve on what the Dean has said; I merely elaborate it in my own words.

it distasteful to submit to herd opinion. History tells them that democracies are far from perfect and have in the past done many foolish and even wicked things. But they do not dispute that in the end the will of the people must prevail nor do they seek to appeal from it to the throne of reason.

But when it comes to a pure point of morals—for example, is homosexuality immoral and sinful?—the first reaction of most of us is different. That reaction illustrates vividly the vacuum that is created when a society no longer acknowledges a supreme spiritual authority. For most of the history of mankind this sort of question has been settled, for men in society as well as for men as individuals, by priests claiming to speak with the voice of God. Today a man's own conscience is for him the final arbiter: but what for society?

This problem does not arise for one who takes the extreme view that society and the law have no concern at all with morals and that a man may behave as he wishes so long as he respects another's physical person and property. But I believe that there is general agreement that that is not enough and that the law should prevent a man from, for example, corrupting the morals of youth or offending the moral standards of others by a public display of what they regard as vice. The law cannot interfere in these ways except from the basis of a common or public morality. Whatever view one takes of the law's right of intervention—whether it should be no wider than is necessary to protect youth or as wide as may be desirable to conserve the moral health of the whole community—one still has to answer the question: 'How are moral standards to be ascertained in the absence of a spiritual authority?'

This question, it seems to me, has received less study than it ought to have. The lawyers have evaded it by means of the assumption, substantially justifiable in fact though not in theory, that Christian morality remains just as valid for the purposes of the law as it was in the days of a universal church. The philosophers seem to have assumed that because a man's conscience could do for him, if he so chose, all that in the age of faith the priest had done, it could likewise do for society all that the priest had done. It cannot, unless some way be found of making up a collective conscience.

It is said or implied that this can be done by accepting the sovereignty of reason which will direct the conscience of every man to the same conclusion. The humbler way of using the power of reason is to hold, as Aquinas did, that through it it is possible to ascertain the law as God ordered it, the natural law, the law as it ought to be; the prouder is to assert that the reason of man unaided can construct the law as it ought to be. If the latter view is right, then one must ask: As men of reason are all men equal? If they are, if every man has equivalent power of reasoning and strength of mind to subdue the baser faculties of feeling and emotion, there can be no objection to morality being a matter for the popular vote. The objection is sustainable only upon the view that the opinion of the trained and educated mind, reached as its owner believes by an unimpassioned rational process, is as a source of morals superior to the opinion of ordinary men.[1]

To the whole of this thesis, however it be put and whether or not it is valid for the individual mind that is governed by philosophy or faith, the law-maker in a democratic society must advance insuperable objections, both practical and theoretical. The practical objection is that after centuries of debate, men of undoubted reasoning power and honesty of purpose have shown themselves unable to agree on what the moral law should be, differing sometimes upon the answer to the simplest moral problem. To say this is not to deny the value of discussion among moral philosophers or to overlook the possibility that sometime between now and the end of the world universal agreement may be reached, but it is to say that as a guide to the degree of definition required by the law-maker the method is valueless. Theoretically the method is inadmissible. If what reason has to discover is the law of God, it is inadmissible because it assumes, as of course Aquinas did, belief in God as a law-giver. If it is the law of man and if a common opinion on any point is held by the educated *élite*, what is obtained except to substitute for the voice of God the voice of the Superior Person? A free society is as much offended by the dictates of an intellectual oligarchy as by those of an autocrat.

For myself I have found no satisfactory alternative to the thesis I have proposed. The opposition to it, I cannot help thinking, has not rid itself of the idea, natural to a philosopher, that a man who is seeking a moral law ought also to be in pursuit of absolute truth. If he were, they would think it surprising if he found truth at the

---

[1] In a letter published in *The Times* (London), 22 March 1961, p. 13, col. 5, a distinguished historian wrote that what clinched the issue in the relationship between morality and the law was 'simply that it is impossible to administer justice on a law as to which there is a fundamental disagreement among *educated* opinion'. (My italics.)

bottom of the popular vote. I do not think it as far from this as some
learned people suppose and I have known them to search for it in
what seem to me to be odder places. But that is a subject outside
the scope of this lecture which is not concerned with absolute truth.
I have said that a sense of right and wrong is necessary for the life of
a community. It is not necessary that their appreciation of right
and wrong, tested in the light of one set or another of those abstract
propositions about which men forever dispute, should be correct.
If it were, only one society at most could survive. What the law-
maker has to ascertain is not the true belief but the common belief.

When I talk of the law-maker I mean a man whose business it is
to make the law whether it takes the form of a legislative enactment
or of a judicial decision, as contrasted with the lawyer whose business
is to interpret and apply the law as it is. Of course the two functions
often overlap; judges especially are thought of as performing both.
No one now is shocked by the idea that the lawyer is concerned
simply with the law as it is and not as he thinks it ought to be. No
one need be shocked by the idea that the law-maker is concerned
with morality as it is. There are, have been, and will be bad laws,
bad morals, and bad societies. Probably no law-maker believes that
the morality he is enacting is false, but that does not make it true.
Unfortunately bad societies can live on bad morals just as well as
good societies on good ones.

In a democracy educated men cannot be put into a separate
category for the decision of moral questions. But that does not mean
that in a free society they cannot enjoy and exploit the advantage of
the superior mind. The law-maker's task, even in a democracy, is not
the drab one of counting heads or of synthesizing answers to moral
questions given in a Gallup poll. In theory a sharp line can be
drawn between law and morality as they are—positive law and
positive morality—and as they ought to be; but in practice no such
line can be drawn, because positive morality, like every other basis
for the law, is subject to change, and consequently the law has to be
developed. A judge is tethered to the positive law but not shackled
to it. So long as he does not break away from the positive law, that
is, from the precedents which are set for him or the clear language
of the statute which he is applying, he can determine for himself
the distance and direction of his advance. Naturally he will move
towards the law as he thinks it ought to be. If he has moved in the
right direction, along the way his society would wish to go, there will

come a time when the tethering-point is uprooted and moved nearer to the position he has taken; if he has moved in the wrong direction, he or his successors will be pulled back.

The legislator as an enforcer of morals has far greater latitude than the modern judge. Legislation of that sort is not usually made an election issue but is left to the initiative of those who are returned to power. In deciding whether or not to take the initiative the relevant question nearly always is not what popular morality is but whether it should be enforced by the criminal law. If there is a reasonable doubt on the first point, that doubt of itself answers the whole question in the negative. The legislator must gauge the intensity with which a popular moral conviction is held, because it is only when the obverse is generally thought to be intolerable that the criminal law can safely and properly be used. But if he decides that point in favour of the proposed legislation, there are many other factors, some of principle and some of expediency, to be weighed, and these give the legislator a wide discretion in determining how far he will go in the direction of the law as he thinks it ought to be. The restraint upon him is that if he moves too far from the common sense of his society, he will forfeit the popular goodwill and risk seeing his work undone by his successor.

This is the method of law-making common to both America and England. The popular vote does not itself enact or veto; rather, the initiative is put into the hands of a very few men. Under this method the law reformer has a double opportunity. He may work upon the popular opinion which is the law-makers' base or he may influence the law-maker directly. At each of these stages the educated man is at an advantage in a democratic society.

Let us consider the first stage. True it is that in the final count the word of the educated man goes for no more than that of any other sort of man. But in the making up of the tally he has or should have the advantage of powers of persuasion above the ordinary. I do not mean by that simply powers of reasoning. If he is to be effective he must be ready to persuade and not just to teach, and he must accept that reason is not the plain man's only guide. 'The common morality of a society at any time', says Dean Rostow, 'is a blend of custom and conviction, of reason and feeling, of experience and prejudice.'[1] If an educated man is armed only with reason, if he is disdainful of custom and ignores strength of feeling, if he

[1] Rostow, op. cit. p. 197.

thinks of 'prejudice' and 'intolerance' as words with no connotations that are not disgraceful and is blind to religious conviction, he had better not venture outside his academy, for if he does he will have to deal with forces he cannot understand. Not all learned men are prepared like Bertrand Russell to sit on the pavement outside No. 10 Downing Street. Not all are lucid as well as erudite. Many a man will find satisfaction in teaching others to do what he is not equipped to do himself; but it is naïve for such a man to reproach judges and legislators for making what he deems to be irrational law, as if in a democratic society they were the agents only of reason and the controllers of a nation's thought.

The other advantage which the educated man possesses is that he has easier access to the ear of the law-maker. I do not mean merely by lobbying. When—with such latitude as our democratic and judicial system allows—the law-maker is determining the pace and direction of his advance from the law that is towards the law that ought to be, he does and should inform himself of the views of wise and experienced men and pay extra attention to them.

These are the ways by which well-informed and articulate men can play a part in the shaping of the law quite disproportionate to their numbers. Under a system in which no single question is submitted to the electorate for direct decision, an ardent minority for or against a particular measure may often count for more than an apathetic majority. Recently in England in the reform of the criminal law a minority has had some remarkable successes. In 1948 flogging was abolished as a judicial punishment;[1] it is doubtful whether that would have been the result of a majority vote, and it is still uncertain whether the gain will be held. Some years later much the same body of opinion was very nearly successful in abolishing capital punishment; I do not believe that in the country as a whole there is a majority against capital punishment. In 1959 the common law on obscenity was altered by statute.[2] Notwithstanding that the tendency of a book is to deprave and corrupt, it is a good defence if its publication is in the interests of some 'object of general concern', such as literature or art; and the opinion of experts is made admissible on the merits of the work. Under this latter provision in the recent case of *Lady Chatterley's Lover*,[3] thirty-five witnesses dis-

[1] Criminal Justice Act, 1948, 11 & 12 Geo. 6, c. 58, s. 2.
[2] Obscene Publications Act, 1959, 7 & 8 Eliz. 2, c. 66, s. 4.
[3] The transcript of the trial, somewhat abridged, has been published as *The Trial of Lady Chatterley : Regina v. Penguin Books Limited* (Rolph edn. 1961).

tinguished in the fields of literature and morals were permitted to discuss at large the merits of the book, and thus a specially qualified body of opinion was brought into direct communication with the jury. On the other hand there has so far been a failure to reform the law against homosexuality. The conclusion of the Wolfenden Committee is an indication—I believe a correct one—that a substantial majority of 'educated opinion' is in favour of some modification; but I believe also that the Home Secretary was right in his conclusion that public opinion as a whole was too strongly against the proposed amendments to permit legislation.

I have been considering this subject on the assumption that the extent to which the moral law is translated into the law of the land is determined chiefly by the legislature. In England that has appeared to be so at any rate during the last hundred years. The law that is now consolidated in the Sexual Offence sAct of 1956[1] is mainly the creation of statute. Incest, for example, the lesser homosexual offences, and carnal knowledge of girls under the age of sixteen were never crimes at common law. Parliament in a series of statutes felt its way cautiously towards the curbing of prostitution, approaching the situation obliquely and at several different angles. The second cardinal enunciation of principle in *Shaw*'s case, to which I must now return, is that in matters of morals the common law has abandoned none of its rights and duties; and the third relates to the function of the jury.

What exactly is meant by a conspiracy to corrupt public morals? We all know what a conspiracy is in law. Since acts of immorality are rarely committed by one person only, it is not in this branch of the law an element of much importance. What limits, if any, are implicit in the words 'public' and 'corrupt'? Is it corruption to offer an adult an opportunity of committing, not for the first time, an immoral act? If so, what element of publicity has there to be about it? In the course of a very strong dissenting speech Lord Reid reached the conclusion that the successful argument by the Crown made 'unlawful every act which tends to lead a single individual morally astray'.[2] Their lordships in the majority refrained —I think, deliberately—from defining their terms. They left the work to the jury. Lord Simonds said: 'The uncertainty that necessarily arises from the vagueness of general words can only be

[1] 4 & 5 Eliz. 2, c. 69.
[2] *Shaw* v. *Director of Public Prosecutions* (1961), *supra* at 278.

resolved by the opinion of twelve chosen men and women.'[1] On the question of what was meant by the words in the indictment Lord Tucker said: 'It is for the jury to construe and apply these words to the facts proved in evidence and reach their own decision. . . .'[2] Lord Morris said: 'Even if accepted public standards may to some extent vary from generation to generation, current standards are in the keeping of juries, who can be trusted to maintain the corporate good sense of the community and to discern attacks upon values that must be preserved.'[3] Lord Hodson said that the function of *custos morum* would ultimately be performed by the jury: '. . . in the field of public morals it will thus be the morality of the man in the jury box that will determine the fate of the accused. . . .'[4]

The opinions in *Shaw*'s case have given rise to much debate. Critics of the majority view complain that it removes from the criminal law on morals the element of reasonable certainty. The relationship between statute and common law surely needs further elucidation. In this respect the immediate impact of the case is sharp. The legislators in Whitehall, inching forward clause by clause towards their moral objectives, topped a rise only to find the flag of their ally, the common law, whom they erroneously believed to be comatose (the Crown cited only three reported cases of conspiracy to corrupt public morals since Lord Mansfield's dictum in 1763), flying over the whole territory, a small part of which they had laboriously occupied.

There is another important aspect of the case, and that is whether, in placing so heavy a burden on the jury, it has brought about a shift of responsibility for decisions in the moral field that affects the democratic process I have endeavoured to describe.

If the only question the jury had to decide was whether or not a moral belief was generally held in the community, the jury would, I think, be an excellent tribunal. It will be objected that the decision

---

[1] *Shaw* v. *Director of Public Prosecutions, supra* at 269.
[2] ibid. at 290.   [3] ibid. at 292.
[4] ibid. at 294. The opinions in *Shaw*'s case were considered by the Court of Criminal Appeal in July 1961, and, with the aid of them, the court approved a definition of what was meant by a 'disorderly house', the premises in question being private premises in which strip-tease performances were exhibited. To constitute an offence, the court held, the exhibition must amount to an outrage of public decency *or* tend to corrupt or deprave, *or* be 'otherwise calculated to injure the public interest so as to call for condemnation and punishment'. *Regina* v. *Quinn* (1961), 3 Weekly L.R. 611, 615 (C.A.). These tests are alternative, and the last of them shows the width of the discretion that is given to the jury.

would not be that of a jury alone but of a jury assisted by a judge; and in the minds of many reformers, some of whom identify liberalism with relaxation, the views of a judge on what is immoral are suspect. It is true that on this question a judge usually takes the conservative view, but so does the British public.

This is, however, as I have now stressed several times, unlikely to be the issue. The argument will not usually be about the immorality of the act but about whether the arm of the law should be used to suppress it. Hitherto the role of the jury has been negative and never formally recognized. The jury resists the enforcement of laws which it thinks to be too harsh. The law has never conceded that it has the right to do that, but it has been accepted that in practice it will exercise its power in that way. The novelty in the dicta in *Shaw*'s case is that they formally confer on the jury a positive function in law enforcement. It cannot be intended that the jury's only duty is to draw the line between public morality and immorality. If, for example, a man and a woman were charged with conspiring to corrupt public morals by openly living in sin, a jury today might be expected to acquit. If homosexuality were to cease to be *per se* criminal and two men were to be similarly charged with flaunting their relationship in public, a jury today might be expected —I think that this is what Lord Simonds and Lord Tucker would contemplate[1]—to convict. The distinction can be made only on the basis that one sort of immorality ought to be condemned and punished and the other not. That is a matter on which many people besides lawyers are qualified to speak and would desire to be heard before a decision is reached. When a minister submits the issue to Parliament, they can be heard; when a judge submits it to a jury, they cannot. The main burden of Lord Reid's trenchant criticism of the majority opinion is that it allows and requires the jury to perform the function of the legislator.

Of course the courts would never deny the supremacy of Parliament. If Parliament dislikes the fruits of the legal process, it can say so; frequently in the past it has altered the law declared by the courts. But in the legislative process the forces of inertia are considerable; and in matters of morals negative legislation is especially difficult, because relaxation is thought to imply approval. So whoever has the initiative has the advantage. For the moment it appears that the common law has regained the initiative.

[1] *Shaw* v. *Director of Public Prosecutions, supra* at 268 and 285.

Whether it retains it or not, *Shaw*'s case settles for the purposes of the law that morality in England means what twelve men and women think it means—in other words, it is to be ascertained as a question of fact. I am not repelled by that phrase nor do I resent in such a matter submission to the mentality of the common man. Those who believe in God and that He made man in His image will believe also that He gave to each in equal measure the knowledge of good and evil, placing it not in the intellect wherein His grant to some was more bountiful than to others, but in the heart and understanding, building there in each man the temple of the Holy Ghost. Those who do not believe in God must ask themselves what they *mean* when they say that they believe in democracy. Not that all men are born with equal brains—we cannot believe that; but that they have at their command—and that in this they are all born in the same degree—the faculty of telling right from wrong. This is the whole meaning of democracy, for if in this endowment men were not equal, it would be pernicious that in the government of any society they should have equal rights.

To hold that morality is a question of fact is not to deify the *status quo* or to deny the perfectibility of man. The unending search for truth goes on and so does the struggle towards the perfect society. It is our common creed that no society can be perfect unless it is a free society; and a free society is one that is created not as an end in itself but as a means of securing and advancing the bounds of freedom for the individuals who live within it. This is not the creed of all mankind. In this world as it is no man can be free unless he lives within the protection of a free society. If a free man needed society for no other reason, he would need it for this, that if he stood alone his freedom would be in peril. In the free society there are men, fighters for freedom, who strain at the bonds of their society, having a vision of life as they feel it ought to be. They live gloriously, and many of them die gloriously, and in life and in death they magnify freedom. What they gain and as they gain it becomes the property of their society and is to be kept. The law is its keeper. So there are others, defenders and not attackers, but also fighters for freedom, for those who defend a free society defend freedom. These others are those who serve the law. They do not look up too often to the heights of what ought to be lest they lose sight of the ground on which they stand and which it is their duty to defend—the law as it is, morality as it is, freedom as it is—none of them perfect but the things that their society has got and must not let go. It is the faith of the English lawyer, as it is of all those other lawyers who took and enriched the law that Englishmen first made, that most of what their societies have got is good. With that faith they serve the law, saying as Cicero said, '*Legum denique . . . omnes servi sumus ut liberi esse possimus*'.[1] In the end we are all of us slaves to the law, for that is the condition of our freedom.

---

[1] Cicero, *Pro A. Cluentio*, 53, 146.

VI

Mill on Liberty in Morals*

John Stuart Mill thought to resolve the struggle between liberty
and authority that is inherent in every society. We who belong to
the societies of the United States or of the British Commonwealth
or of other like-minded peoples say that we belong to a free society.
By this I think we mean no more than that we strike a balance in
favour of individual freedom. The law is the boundary that marks
the limit of authority and it is not drawn in a straight line. As it
traverses the field of human activities it inclines from side to side, in
some allowing much more freedom than in others. At each point we
try to strike the right balance. What I mean by striking it in favour
of freedom is that the question to be asked in each case is: 'How
much authority is necessary?' and not: 'How much liberty is to be
conceded?' That the question should be put in that form, that
authority should be a grant and liberty not a privilege, is, I think, the
true mark of a free society.

Is it possible to drive a straight line across the field running from
one end to the other, marking out for all time the private domain
on one side and the public on the other? If it is, the value to the
individual in the minority would be immense. As things are, in the
constant struggle between liberty and authority the individual is at
a disadvantage. Each time the Government, backed by the power of
the majority, brings forward some new piece of legislation designed
to benefit the majority and involving some further invasions of the
private domain, the minority can only appeal to an undefined concept of liberty. Lack of definition suits the stronger party. What is
wanted, if it can be got, is a comprehensive principle, clear and
precise, by which any proposed law can be tested.

This sort of thing—the idea of formulating a law above ordinary
law and by which ordinary law may be tested, is attempted on a

* The Ernst Freund Lecture delivered at the University of Chicago on 15 October
1964 and printed in the *University of Chicago Law Review*, vol. 32, No. 2.

grand scale in the Constitution of the United States. The scale was
not grand enough for Mill. The Constitution was built to be permanent: Mill's doctrine was designed as perdurable. The Articles of
the Constitution were made difficult to alter, but Mill dealt in
immutabilities. No society, he said,[1] in which the liberties which he
prescribed were not on the whole respected was free, whatever
might be its form of government; and none was completely free in
which they did not exist absolutely and unqualified. Again, where the
Constitution protects only specific freedoms, such as the freedom to
exercise religion, freedom of speech and of the press, and so forth,
Mill induced from the specific freedoms he enumerated a definition
wide enough to cover all freedom. He regarded the Constitution as
inadequate. The fact that in his day 'nearly half the United States
have been interdicted by law from making any use whatever of
fermented drinks, except for medical purposes' was placed first in
his list of 'gross usurpations upon the liberty of private life'.[2] What
Mill declared was a fundamental doctrine, to be kept as in a taber-
nacle in the hearts of men, to which all law, including the law that
makes and amends constitutions, should be subject.

Mill therefore set out to define once and for all 'the nature and
limits of the power which can be legitimately exercised by society
over the individual'.[3] He did this by asserting 'one very simple
principle, as entitled to cover absolutely the dealings of society with
the individual in the way of compulsion and control. . . . That
principle is, that the sole end for which mankind are warranted,
individually or collectively, in interfering with the liberty of action
of any of their number, is self-protection. That the only purpose
for which power can be rightfully exercised over any member of a
civilised community, against his will, is to prevent harm to others.
His own good, either physical or moral, is not a sufficient warrant.
He cannot rightfully be compelled to do or forbear because it will be
better for him to do so, because it will make him happier, because, in
the opinion of others, to do so would be wise, or even right.'[4]

The core of this principle is that a man must be allowed to pursue
his own good in his own way. Its opposite has come to be identified
as paternalism. But an identifying mark is not a line. To secure the
citadel of freedom Mill flung a line beyond which the law must not
trespass. The law was not to interfere with a man unless what he

[1] Mill, *On Liberty*, p. 75.
[2] ibid. p. 144.
[3] ibid. p. 65.
[4] ibid. p. 72.

did caused harm to others. What Mill included in 'harm to others' was chiefly physical harm to other individuals.

Now if a man lives in society it is not simply his own concern whether or not he keeps himself physically, mentally, and morally fit. He owes in these respects a duty to others as well as to himself. Mill accepted the duty as owing to 'assignable individuals', such as a man's family or his creditors. He did not see it as a debt due to society at large. The only right he allowed to society as a collective entity, i.e., to the State, and which it might enforce by law, was the right to exact contributions to common defence and protection. 'But with regard to the merely contingent, or, as it may be called, constructive injury which a person causes to society, by conduct which neither violates any specific duty to the public, nor occasions perceptible hurt to any assignable individual except himself, the inconvenience is one which society can afford to bear, for the sake of the greater good of human freedom.'[1]

Yet if apart from his assignable duties a man does not observe some standard of health and morality, society as a whole is impoverished, for such a man puts less than his share into the common well-being. The enforcement of an obligation of this sort can be distinguished from paternalism. The motive of paternalism is to do good to the individual: the motive of the other is to prevent the harm that would be done to society by the weakness or vice of too many of its members. Mill did not overlook the distinction; he overrode it in the interests of individual freedom. If a man knew his own true interest and pursued it as he ought to, he would make himself as virtuous as he could and by so doing make his contribution to society's well-being. The right to exact such a contribution must be sacrificed on the altar of freedom. If Mill had said otherwise, his doctrine would have lost its definition. It is one thing to distinguish between the duty a man owes to himself to keep fit and the like duty which he owes to society, and it is another thing to define the borderline between them. Grant to society the right in its own interest to tell individuals how they should behave and at once the citadel is under attack. You cannot draw a line which keeps the intervention of the State to the minimum; you can only beg it to remember why it is there and urge it not to go too far.

As Mill noted,[2] this conception of liberty was not accepted in his own time which we now look back upon as an age of individualism

[1] Mill, *On Liberty*, p. 138.		[2] ibid. p. 76.

triumphant. In the hundred years that have passed since then it has over and over again been decisively rejected in economic matters. Its weakness in practice is that it enables one man in a hundred to hold up indefinitely projects which would benefit the other ninety-nine. So we have laws that allow the compulsory acquisition of property. We have also social schemes that an individual is not allowed to contract out of because he cannot be excluded from the benefits of the scheme without wrecking it. Contracting out may be an expression of individuality and proceed from the pure desire for liberty, but we have come to think that it proceeds from selfishness or laziness, indifference to the common good, or a desire to get something for nothing. So we have health laws, thinking it wrong that a man should receive the benefit of modern sanitation in the town in which he lives and keep his own home as a pigsty.

In short, the great majority of our fellow citizens may be as high-minded as Mill expected them to be but we have not yet got rid of the troublesome minority who will yield only to compulsion. Perhaps in the course of several centuries, teaching and example will lift the minority to the common level and in the end it might have been better for us all if we had waited for that to happen. But social reformers are not as patient as philosophers and we have not waited.

This does not mean that necessarily we have witnessed the triumph of paternalism. We would still, I think, most of us deeply resent a law that was passed avowedly for our own good and treated us as if we were in need of care and protection. What it means is that the citadel has not been secured from attack in the way in which Mill proposed. His outer line enclosed territory which has had to be yielded, and authority has not decisively, as he hoped, been kept at bay.

The incident in England which has recently revived interest in Mill's doctrine is the publication of the Wolfenden Report in 1957. The Report based its proposals for the reform of criminal law on homosexuality upon the principle of the realm of private morality which is not the law's business. This use of the principle is, as Professor Hart observed,[1] 'strikingly similar' to Mill's doctrine. Professor Hart immediately conferred upon it his full approval with all the authority which that carries and in 1963 devoted a series of comprehensive and penetrating lectures to expounding it. The idea that in a free society a man's morals should be his own affair is

[1] Hart, *Law, Liberty and Morality*, p. 14.

superficially at least an attractive one. We have built a society in which a man's religion is his own affair: can we not go a step further and build one in which his morals are his own affair too? The law knows nothing of any religion. Is there any need for it to know anything of morals?

Let me for a moment stop talking about society as an abstract conception and talk instead about a hundred men and women. Ninety are virtuous and ten are vicious. Are the virtuous to be compelled to associate with the vicious? The natural answer is—certainly not. For even granted that the vicious do no physical harm to others against their will, association with them may cause the vice to be spread. Moreover, the object of the association being to share the burdens and benefits of life among the community as a whole, it is likely that the vicious will be more benefited than burdened; men who are constantly drunk, drugged or debauched are not likely to be useful members of the community.

What then are the ninety to do about it? If all that was involved was the membership of a social club, the situation would be simple. The vicious ten would be expelled and no one would think the expulsion harsh. But a society in which a man has his whole social life is something more than a club. Men can no longer be driven into the desert; outlawry and banishment are things of the past. Even when in use they were as punishments so severe that mercy enjoined, at least at first, a lesser penalty. Is it therefore permissible for the ninety to deprive the ten of their liberty for the purpose at best of reformation and at worst of restraint? Or must they in the name of freedom leave the ten at large, relying on the strength of their own virtue to resist contamination and in time to convert the vicious?

I do not suppose that any secular society has ever existed which sought to control vice simply by passive resistance and good works. But this is what Mill's conception of a free society demands. Mill's opinion of what was virtuous did not substantially differ from that of his contemporaries. But no one, he felt, could be sure. In a free society full scope must be given to individuality as one of the elements of well-being and the individual must be free to question, challenge and experiment. 'The liberty of the individual must be thus far limited; he must not make himself a nuisance to other people. But if he refrains from molesting others in what concerns them, and merely acts according to his own inclination and judgement in things which concern himself, the same reasons which show that opinion should be free, prove also that he should be allowed, without molestation, to carry his opinions into practice at his own cost. That mankind are not infallible; that their truths, for the most part, are only half-truths; that unity of opinion, unless resulting from the fullest and freest comparison of opposite opinions, is not desirable, and diversity not an evil, but a good, until mankind are much more capable than at present of recognising all sides of the truth, are principles applicable to men's modes of action, not less than to their opinions. As it is useful that while mankind are imperfect there should be different opinions, so it is that there should be different experiments of living; that free scope should be given to varieties of character, short of injury to others; and that the worth of different modes of life should be proved practically, when anyone thinks fit to try them.'[1]

It is with freedom of opinion and discussion that Mill is primarily concerned. Freedom of action follows naturally on that; men must be allowed to do what they are allowed to talk about doing. Evidently what Mill visualizes is a number of people doing things he himself would disapprove of, but doing them earnestly and openly and after thought and discussion in an endeavour to find the way of life best suited to them as individuals. This seems to me on the whole an idealistic picture. It has happened to some extent in the growth of free love. Although for many it is just the indulgence of the flesh, for some it is a serious decision to break the constraint of chastity outside marriage. In the area of morals touched by the law I find it difficult to think of any other example of high-mindedness. A man does not as a rule commit bigamy because he wants to experiment with two wives instead of one. He does not as a rule lie with his daughter or sister because he thinks that an incestuous relationship can be a good one but because he finds in it a way of satisfying his lust in the home. He does not keep a brothel so as to prove the value of promiscuity but so as to make money. There must be some homosexuals who believe theirs to be a good way of life but many more who would like to get free of it if only they could. Certainly no one in his senses can think that habitual drunkenness or drugging leads to any good at all.

Such are the vices that the law seeks to control. If the ninety men, who sincerely believe all this to be depravity, are to be convinced

[1] Mill, p. 114.

that they must put up with it in their society because after all they are not infallible, their truths may be only half-truths, and that it is only by diversity of precept and practice that the whole truth can be found, surely they must be persuaded that there is at least one man among the ten seeking after the truth and proclaiming that what is commonly received as a vice is in truth a virtue. Freedom is not a good in itself. We believe it to be good because out of freedom there comes more good than bad. If a free society is better than a disciplined one, it is because—and this certainly was Mill's view—it is better for a man himself that he should be free to seek his own good in his own way and better too for the society to which he belongs, since thereby a way may be found to a greater good for all. But no good can come from a man doing what he acknowledges to be evil. The freedom that is worth having is freedom to do what you think to be good notwithstanding that others think it to be bad. Freedom to do what you know to be bad is worthless.

Mill believed that diversity in morals and the removal of restraint on what was traditionally held to be immorality would liberate men to prove what they thought to be good. He would have been the last man to have advocated the removal of restraint so as to permit self-indulgence. He conceived of an old morality being replaced by a new and perhaps better morality; he would not have approved of those who did not care whether there was any morality at all. But he did not really grapple with the fact that along the paths that depart from traditional morals, pimps leading the weak astray far outnumber spiritual explorers at the head of the strong. It is significant that when Mill touched on this problem—the commercialization of vice —his teaching wavered.

Should a person, he asked,[1] be free to be a pimp or to keep a gambling-house? Against the affirmative answer which flows logically from his doctrine, Mill put the following argument. If society believes conduct to be bad, it must be at least a disputable question whether it is good or bad: that being so, society is entitled to exclude the influence of solicitations which are not disinterested. There was, he thought, considerable force in this argument and he would not venture to decide the point.

But there are other reasons than a desire to make money which may make a person indulge in vice and solicit others to join with him. Disinterestedness is not proved because money is not

[1] Mill, p. 154.

demanded. Mill's doctrine caters bountifully for good men who are unorthodox. The only bad men he sees at his table are those who are trading in vice and then he does not quite know what to do with them. I think that the true distinction does not lie between those who trade in vice and those who do not, but between those who practise what they know to be vice and those who practise what they believe to be virtue. Only the latter are truly disinterested.

Let us suppose that in the mass of the iniquitous there are some righteous and disinterested men. If then the law is used to suppress immorality, it may suppress also new morality which its advocates sincerely claim to be better than the old. The suppression of any new beliefs sincerely held and purposefully translated into action is injurious to a free society. On this two questions arise. First, can the wheat be separated from the chaff, the chaff burnt, and the wheat made into bread? If not, how is the injury done to society by the suppression of a new morality to be balanced against the injury done by the toleration of acknowledged vice?

I shall begin with the second question because Mill's disciples think that they have an easy answer to it which will make it unnecessary to trouble about the first. Their answer is that the toleration of acknowledged vice, provided that it is confined to private immorality, does not injure society at all; or that if it does, the law is useless as an instrument for suppression. So there is no need for separation and nothing to balance. It may be disagreeable for the ninety virtuous men to have to associate with the vicious ones, or at least to have to extend the benefit and protection of their society to those who are undeserving of it; but that, as Mill says in the passage I have quoted, is an inconvenience which society can afford to bear for the sake of the greater good of human freedom.

The twin arguments that the law is useless against private immorality and that the damage done by private immorality to society is insignificant, have much in common. One thing that they have in common is that their supporters tend, consciously or unconsciously, to apply them in particular to one sort of private immorality which is now much in the public notice, namely, homosexuality between consenting adults. It is argued that the enforcement of the laws against homosexuals causes great misery to men who are morally incapable of changing their way of life. The argument has in this instance an appeal which it altogether lacks when applied to pimps and brothel-keepers. Their supporters tend also, consciously or unconsciously, to forget that what is in dispute is not whether a particular law should be on the statute book but whether it is a condition of a free society that private immorality should altogether and always be immune from interference by the law. No one suggests that all private immorality should be punished by the law as a matter of course. You can grant that private immorality is within the competence of the legislature in a free society and still advance many powerful arguments why the law should not try to punish particular vices in particular circumstances. But if you want to sustain your arguments for reform in a particular case by invoking a principle that exempts all private immorality always from the operation of the law, you put yourself at a disadvantage in two respects. First, it is for your opponents and not for you to select examples by which to test the validity of the principle. You have undertaken to show that it is good for all private immorality. Secondly, even when you are dealing with a particular vice, it is not enough for you to show that in a given society at a given time it is not practised extensively enough to do appreciable injury. You have to show that the vice is not of its nature one that is capable of injuring society. Only then can society safely sign away its power of control.

If these considerations are kept clearly in mind, I think that the arguments I am about to examine will lose much of their superficial attractiveness. Indeed, I think that I can dispose of one of them very shortly. It is true that, as Professor Hart says,[1] morality is not best taught by fear of legal punishment; and it may be that a conformity, which is motivated mainly by that fear, is not a value worth pursuing. But the law does not intervene merely to punish or to deter but also to give opportunity for reform; and it is not concerned simply with the good of the individual who is being punished. It is concerned as much or more with the good of those who might be led into evil by example or temptation. If the evildoer himself is beyond reform, the threat of punishment may deter and to that extent prevent the spread of the vice; or if beyond deterrence, imprisonment can at least put him out of the way of others he might influence.

I do not understand the distinction in this respect between crimes of private immorality and other crimes. If it is useless to fine or imprison people for peddling pornography, why is it sensible

[1] Hart, pp. 57-58.

to punish them for burglary or rape? Certainly it is right to weigh the advantages which imprisonment may be expected to achieve— not only for the criminal but also and primarily for those who might otherwise suffer from him—against the misery it inflicts. But that is a consideration going to the weight with which the law should come down upon the criminal; it is not an argument for its exclusion. The misery of an incurable homosexual imprisoned because he cannot keep away from small boys is no less than that of one (there may still be a few in England) who is imprisoned for offences with adults; and if the law is useless in the latter case, what is its value in the former in which it is admitted that it can properly be employed? Then if one turns to the grosser forms of vice, it appears to me to be contrary to common sense to assert that fines and imprisonment are useless weapons against those whose only interest in the vice racket is for what they can get out of it.

Granted then that the law can play some part in the war against vice, ought it to be excluded for the reason that private vice cannot do any harm to society? I think that it is capable of doing both physical harm and spiritual harm. Tangible and intangible may be better words; body and soul a better simile.

Let me consider first the tangible harm. It is obvious that an individual may by unrestricted indulgence in vice so weaken himself that he ceases to be a useful member of society. It is obvious also that if a sufficient number of individuals so weaken themselves, society will thereby be weakened. That is what I mean by tangible harm to society. If the proportion grows sufficiently large, society will succumb either to its own disease or to external pressure. A nation of debauchees would not in 1940 have responded satisfactorily to Winston Churchill's call to blood and toil and sweat and tears. I doubt if any of this would be denied. The answer that is made to it is that the danger, if private immorality were tolerated, of vice spreading to such an extent as to affect society as a whole is negligible and in a free society ought to be ignored.

There is here a distinction to be made. As I have said, the question is not whether at any given time the spread of a particular vice has reached such proportions as to constitute a danger, but whether all vice that can be committed in private is of its nature harmless to society. It is therefore proper to distinguish between natural and unnatural vice; and it is usually an example, such as homosexuality, selected from unnatural vice that is taken to illustrate the absurdity of supposing that private immorality could ever develop into a menace to society. Of course, looking at the thing in the crudest way, a completely homosexual society would, unless continuously reinforced from outside, soon cease to exist because it would not breed. But, as has been pointed out,[1] the same might be said of a completely celibate society, yet no one regards celibacy as injurious to society. The natural demand for heterosexual intercourse, it is argued, will always be strong enough to ensure that homosexuality is kept to a harmless minority.

This is, within limits, a formidable argument and I shall return to consider the curious results which flow from it. It does not however apply to natural vice where the pressure is the other way. There may be those who argue that men and women are inherently virtuous so that the vicious few, even if allowed free rein, will always be in a harmless and unattractive minority. This seems to me like arguing that the vast majority of men and women in society are inherently loyal so that it would be quite safe to ignore the treacherous few. No doubt traitors, as also vice-mongers, are often in it only for money and no one would applaud that. But there are noble as well as ignoble traitors; and—it might well be argued on the lines of Mill—it is worth putting up with the almost negligible harm that is caused by treachery as it is ordinarily practised so as to make sure that we do not stifle some new political conception, which although now regarded with abhorrence by all right-minded people, may in the end, because we are all fallible, turn out to be a great improvement. The danger that some traitors or spies may deliver up to the enemy some vital secrets is, it can be urged, an imaginary one existing only in story books. In real life the damage they do, at any rate in peacetime, is hardly likely to do more than dent the structure of a strong society.

But this is not the way in which treachery is considered. We do not estimate the achievements of treason over the last century and ask what they have amounted to. So with incitement to mutiny; we do not ask how much can safely be permitted without seriously endangering the discipline of the armed forces. So with sedition; we do not argue that the loyalty of the robust majority and its belief in the merits of our polity is all that is necessary for the safety of the realm. When we are constitution-making—whether what is being formulated is a clause in writing or a principle supported by

[1] See the article by Dr. Mewett listed in the bibliography, p. xiii.

tacit consent—it is the nature of the subject-matter that is the determinant. Whether society should have the power to restrain any activity depends on the nature of the activity. Whether it should exercise the power at any given time in its history depends on the situation at that time and requires a balance to be struck between the foreseeable danger to society and the foreseeable damage to the freedom and happiness of the individual.

This distinction, which one might with some exaggeration call a distinction between eternity and time, is the answer to a modified and more attractive way of putting the argument I have just been considering.[1] Granted that society cannot allow private vice to rampage, ought not its power of interference be confined to the excess? It is, it can be urged, only the excess that is dangerous. It is indeed with this in mind that anti-vice laws are generally framed, that is, to contain rather than to eliminate the vice. It is considered impracticable to use the law to eliminate fornication or even prostitution; the criminal law against soliciting, procuring, living on immoral earnings, and running brothels is designed to keep the vice within limits. But there is no Plimsoll line which can define the safety level.

In the same way, while a few people getting drunk in private cause no problem at all, widespread drunkenness, whether in private or public, would create a social problem. The line between drunkenness that creates a social problem of sufficient magnitude to justify the intervention of the law and that which does not, cannot be drawn on the distinction between private indulgence and public sobriety. It is a practical one, based on an estimate of what can safely be tolerated whether in public or in private, and shifting from time to time as circumstances change. The licensing laws coupled with high taxation may be all that is needed. But if more be needed there is no doctrinal answer even to complete prohibition. It cannot be said that so much is the law's business but more is not.

I move now to the consideration of intangible harm to society and begin by noting a significant distinction. When considering tangible damage to society we are concerned chiefly with immoral activity. Moral belief is relevant only in so far as the lack of it contributes to immoral activity. A vicious minority diminishes the physical strength of society even if all its members believe themselves to be sinning. But if they all believed that, they would not

---

[1] See the article by Dr. Mewett listed in the bibliography p. xiii.

diminish the common belief in right and wrong which is the intangible property of society. When considering intangible injury to society it is moral belief that matters; immoral activity is relevant only in so far as it promotes disbelief.

It is generally accepted that some shared morality, that is, some common agreement about what is right and what is wrong, is an essential element in the constitution of any society.[1] Without it there would be no cohesion. But polygamy can be as cohesive as monogamy and I am prepared to believe that a society based on free love and a community of children could be just as strong (though according to our ideas it could not be as good) as one based on the family. What is important is not the quality of the creed but the strength of the belief in it. The enemy of society is not error but indifference.

On this reasoning there is nothing inherently objectionable about the change of an old morality for a new one. Why then is the law used to guard existing moral beliefs? It is because an old morality cannot be changed for a new morality as an old coat for a new one. The old belief must be driven out by disbelief. Polygamy could not be established in England or in the United States unless there was first created a disbelief in the value of monogamy. If change is in progress there will for a long period be no common belief in the value of either institution. Disbelief in the virtue of chastity is not confined to those who from the purest motives would like to help spinsters to lead a fuller life; and through the breach in the walls made by the new moralist there will come pouring a horde which he would loathe and despise. Whether the new belief is better or worse than the old, it is the interregnum of disbelief that is perilous. During the interregnum, society will be attacked by forces which those, who in the course of their rational discussions have generated the disbelief, will have no power to control and which will be as hostile to the new belief as to the old.

But no one, it will be said, wants to subvert a whole morality. All that is sought is freedom to make peripheral changes or, if not quite peripheral, changes that will leave the bulk of morality intact; nothing will be done that will seriously diminish the cohesive force of a common morality. That brings us back to the old difficulty: how much can be allowed and how can it be measured? If it is proper and indeed necessary for the law to guard some part of public morality, how shall we determine what part to leave unguarded?

[1] See Hart, p. 51.

There is in this respect a special difficulty due to the nature of moral belief. It is not for most men based on a number of separate rational judgements arrived at after weighing the arguments for and against chastity, for and against honesty, for and against homosexuality, and so on. Most men take their morality as a whole and in fact derive it, though this is irrelevant, from some religious doctrine. To destroy the belief in one part of it will probably result in weakening the belief in the whole. Professor Hart says that to argue in this way is to treat morality as if it 'forms a single seamless web'[1] which he finds unconvincing. Seamlessness presses the simile rather hard but, apart from that, I should say that for most people morality is a web of beliefs rather than a number of unconnected ones. This may or may not be the most rational way of arriving at a moral code. But when considering the degree of injury to a public morality, what has to be considered is how the morality is in fact made up and not how in the opinion of rational philosophers it ought to be made up.

But then if the law is required to guard the whole of public morality, is that not, as Professor Hart puts it graphically, using 'legal punishment to freeze into immobility the morality dominant at a particular time in a society's existence'?[2] I do not see why it should have that effect. At the worst it leaves morality as mobile as the law; and though it may not be easy to change the law, it is far easier than to change a moral belief of a community. In fact, for practical reasons the law never attempts to cover the whole of public morality and the area left uncovered is naturally that which is most susceptible to change. But assume that it did cover the whole of public morality, its effect would be not to freeze but to regulate the process of liquefaction and to help distinguish the changes which are motivated by a genuine search after moral improvement from those which are relaxation into vice. It is in this way that the law acts as a winnower, if I may return to the metaphor of the wheat and the chaff. Admittedly it is an unscientific way. There is no phased programme, no planners to say that if free love is let in in the 60's, the homosexualist must wait until the 70's. But relaxation, if it seems to be going too far, sets off a movement for tightening up what is left. The law is brought in to do the tightening as well as to hold off the evil-doers who flourish whenever moral principle is uncertain. A detached observer, who favoured neither the old nor

[1] Hart, p. 51.
[2] ibid. p. 72.

the new morality, would see this as a natural, albeit a rough and ready, method of regulation.

In any society in which the members have a deeply-rooted desire for individual freedom—and where there is not that desire, it is useless to devise methods for securing it—there is also a natural respect for opinions that are sincerely held. When such opinions accumulate enough weight, the law must either yield or it is broken. In a democratic society, especially one like ours in which laymen play a conspicuous part in the enforcement of the law, there will be a strong tendency for it to yield—not to abandon all defences so as to let in the horde, but to give ground to those who are prepared to fight for something that they prize. To fight may be to suffer. A willingness to suffer is the most convincing proof of sincerity. Without the law there would be no proof. The law is the anvil on which the hammer strikes.

Much of what I have just said is more appropriate to a society in which freedom is still young than to ours. In England today there is no question of the law being used to suppress any activity which is not generally thought to be immoral. The climate of a free society is naturally clement to individuality of any sort and uncongenial to compulsion, so that the criminal law will withdraw its support, if it has ever given it, from a moral belief which is seriously challenged.

It may be that in the case of homosexuality this is too sweeping a statement. I do not think that there is anyone who asserts vocally that homosexuality is a good way of life but there may be those who believe it to be so. This brings me back to the point where I left that subject when distinguishing between natural and unnatural vice. That distinction does not affect the intangible harm that immorality does to society but it is relevant, I suggested, to assessing the likelihood of tangible injury. If the intangible harm is ignored, there is a strong case for arguing that homosexuality between adults should be excluded altogether from the ambit of the law on the ground that as a practice it is incapable of causing appreciable injury to society. I cannot say more than that there is a strong case, for many would argue that homosexuality if tolerated would spread to significant proportions. If one ignores that argument as well, the result would be that the charter of freedom should not encompass the whole of morality but only so much of it as is concerned with unnatural vice—freedom of morality in matters unnatural.

Is this the sort of result that is really worth striving for on a high theoretical plane? Any law reformer who raises this sort of issue must be the sort of man who likes to bang his head against a brick wall in the hope that he will be able to get through on his own terms and so avoid a little argument at the gate. It will not improve his chances of getting through the gate if he tells the janitor that there ought not to be a wall there at all. So it is much easier to obtain the repeal of a law by persuading the law-maker that on balance it is doing more harm than good than by denouncing him as a meddler who ought to be minding his own business.

Whether or not I am right in thinking that this is the only way in which the case for reform can be put, it is certainly the most attractive way. It is put thus cogently by Professor Hart in the preface to his book where, after mentioning proposals for the reform of the law on abortion, homosexuality, and euthanasia, he refers to them as cases where 'the misery caused directly and indirectly by legal punishment outweighs any conceivable harm these practices may do'.[1] This is the balancing process. There are other factors besides human misery (which inevitably accompanies any serious punishment for any breach of the law) to be taken into account; and in my first lecture I enumerated some which it seemed to me the law-maker, whether it be a parliamentary majority or a monarch, ought to weigh before it uses its powers. This applies to every exercise of the criminal law. If the law on abortion causes unnecessary misery, let it be amended, not abolished on the ground that abortion is not the law's business. So with obscenity. It is one thing to amend the law, if we can, so that it will distinguish more effectively between art and obscenity, and another thing to remove altogether the restraint of the law, admitting a flood of pornography, so as to make quite sure that no creative work is left outside. In all these cases the appointed law-makers of society have the duty to balance conflicting values—the value of diversity against the value of conformity—and to form a judgement according to the merits of each case. They cannot be constrained by rule. They cannot suffer a definite limitation on their powers. They cannot be denied entry into some private realm.

It can be said in general terms, and often is, that law-makers are bound to legislate for the common good.[2] The common good is perhaps a useful and compendious, if vague, description of all the things law-makers should have in mind when they legislate. But it

[1] Hart, Preface.   [2] See Dr. St. John-Stevas at p. 37.

does not constitute a clear limitation on the right to legislate. There may be a difference of opinion about what is for the common good which can be solved only by a judgement upon the conflicting values. Society alone can make that judgement and if it makes it honestly, it is a judgement that cannot be impugned.

Can then the judgement of society sanction every invasion of a man's privacy, however extreme? Theoretically that must be so; there is no theoretical limitation. Society must be the judge of what is necessary to its own integrity if only because there is no other tribunal to which the question can be submitted. In a free society the understanding that men have with each other is that each shall retain for himself the greatest measure of personal freedom that is compatible with the integrity and good government of his society. In a free society men must trust each other and each man must put his trust in his fellows that they will not interfere with him unless in their honest judgement it is necessary to do so. Furthermore, in a free society checks are usually put upon the government, both the executive and the legislature, so that it is difficult for them to enact and enforce a law that takes away another's freedom unless in the honest judgement of society it is necessary to do so. One sort of check consists in the safeguarding of certain specific freedoms by the articles of a constitution; another consists in trial by jury. But the only certain security is the understanding in the heart of every man that he must not condemn what another does unless he honestly considers that it is a threat to the integrity or good government of their society.

If one man practises what he calls virtue and the others call vice and if he fails to convince the others that they are wrong, he has the right to make a further appeal. He has, in a free society, a right to claim that however much the others dislike and deplore what he does, they should allow him to do it unless they are genuinely convinced that it threatens the integrity of society. If the others reject that appeal, constitutionally that is the end. He must either submit or reject society.

But suppose he cannot bring himself to believe that the others have formed an honest judgement and holds that as law-makers they have abused their power. He can then in the last resort transfer the issue from the field of law to that great battlefield on which the struggle for human freedom has so often in the past been fought out, a field in which man-made law is overridden and mastery is gained by strength of spirit and depth of conviction. 'An *imperium* there always must be in the State's *imperio* so long as a man retains a conscience and free will.'[1]

But when a man proclaims his own *imperium*, he rebels. The law knows nothing of the right, and it may be the duty, to rebel and cannot recognize it. And since I am talking only about the relationship between law and morals I cannot here concern myself with it. What I have said, I say to show that I am not under the delusion that the law has the ultimate answer to every moral problem and I am not asserting that there is in all circumstances a moral obligation to obey the law. There may be times in the future, as there have been in the past, when a man has to set himself up against society. But if he does so, he must expect to find the law on the side of society. If in his struggle he is armed with a good conscience, he must put his trust, firstly, in the rightness of his conviction, secondly, in the knowledge that nothing that law-makers and lawyers can do can fetter the mind of man, only his body; and last but not least, in the certainty that law can be made effective only through human agents and that a law that is truly tyrannical will not for long command the services of free men.

It was in this way in the past that our ancestors established freedom of religion. To do that they had to destroy the web of medieval thought and that was accomplished no more easily than the triumph of Christianity over paganism. Mill records[2] how the Emperor Marcus Aurelius, whom he considered to be one of the best and greatest of world rulers, tender, enlightened, and humane, persecuted Christianity because existing society, as he saw it, was held together by belief in and reverence of the received divinities. The struggle in the sixteenth century between revealed religion and freedom of conscience was of the same order and entailed as much suffering. How could it be otherwise? Men could not tolerate a heretic so long as they believed that he and all those whom he perverted were doomed to an eternity of Hell. Those societies such as ours which are now founded upon freedom in religious belief are viable because we accept that there is more than one way to the goodness that many call God. Diversity in religious belief and practice is no longer injurious to a society that is so constituted.

But the removal of religion from the structure of society does not mean that a society can exist without faith. There is faith in moral

---

[1] Cardinal Newman, quoted in E. E. Y. Hayes, *Letters to the Duke of Norfolk*, p. 325.
[2] Mill, p. 87.

belief as well as in religious belief. Though it is less precise and less demanding, it is not necessarily less intense. In our societies we believe in the advance of man towards a goal and this belief is the mainspring of our morals. We believe that at some time in the history of mankind, whether on a sudden by a divine stroke or imperceptibly in evolution over millennia, there were extracted from the chaos of the primeval mind concepts of justice, benevolence, mercy, continence, and others of that ilk which we call virtues. The distinction between virtue and vice, between good and evil so far as it affects our actions, is what morals are about. A common religious faith means that there is common agreement about the end of man. A common moral faith means that there is common agreement about the way he should go. A band of travellers can go forward together without knowing what they will find at the end of the journey but they cannot keep in company if they do not journey in the same direction.

Diversity in moral belief and practice would be no more injurious to a society which had no common morality than the like diversity in religious matters is to a society with no common religion. But Mill and his disciples do not conceive of a society without a common morality, if indeed it is conceivable. If they did, if they wanted a society in which morality is as free as religion, they would be faint-hearted in what they preached. They could not then sensibly permit the law, as they do, to punish the corruption of youth or public acts of indecency. Where there is freedom of religion, the conversion of a youth is not thought of as corruption; men would have thought of it as that in the Middle Ages just as we now think of the introduction of a youth to homosexual practices as corruption and not as conversion. Where there is truly freedom of religion, it would be thought intolerant to object to a religious ceremony in a public place on the ground that it was offensive to have brought to one's attention the exhibition of a faith which one thought false and pernicious. Why then do we object to the public exhibition of a false morality and call it indecency? If we thought that unrestricted indulgence in the sexual passions was as good a way of life as any other for those who liked it, we should find nothing indecent in the practice of it either in public or in private. It would become no more indecent than kissing in public. Decency as an objective depends on the belief in continence as a virtue which requires sexual activity to be kept within prescribed bounds.

These reflections show the gulf that separates the religious toleration we have achieved from the moral toleration that Mill wanted. The former is practicable because, while each man believes that his own religion, or the lack of it, is the truth or nearest to the truth, he looks upon the alternatives as lesser good and not as evil. What Mill demands is that we must tolerate what we know to be evil and what no one asserts to be good. He does not ask that in particular cases we should extend tolerance out of pity: he demands that we should cede it for ever as a right. Because it is evil we may protect youth from corruption by it, but save for that we must allow it to spread unhindered by the law and infect the minds of all those who are not strong enough to resist it. Why do ninety of us have to grant this licence to the other ten or, it would be truer to say, ninety-nine to the other one? Because, the answer is, we are fallible. We are all quite convinced that what we call vice is evil but we may be mistaken. Although no one asserts that it is not evil, yet we may be mistaken. True it is that if the waters of toleration are poured upon the muck, bad men will wallow in the bog; but it may be—how can we tell otherwise?—that it is only under such conditions that seed may flourish which some day some good man may bring to fruit and that otherwise the world would lose and be the poorer for it.

This is the kernel of Mill's freedom. This is why we must not suppress vice. It is not because it is not evil; Mill thought that it was. It is not because legal suppression would be futile; this argument, favoured by some of Mill's followers, is not one that he advanced. Nor because Mill thought that in the battle between virtue and vice, virtue would be bound to triumph without the aid of the law. In some cogent passages[1] he refuted the argument that in spite of persecution truth would always prevail against error; and if truth can be suppressed, so can error and so can vice. When all this is stripped away, the kernel of Mill is just this—that he beseeches us to think it possible that we may be mistaken. Because of this possibility, Mill demanded almost absolute freedom for the individual to go his own way, the only function of society being to provide for him an ordered framework within which he might experiment in thought and in action secure from physical harm.

There is here, I humbly believe, a flaw in Mill's thinking which, even assuming that we accept his ideal, renders it unacceptable to the

[1] Mill, p. 89.

law-maker as a basis for action. It lies in the failure to distinguish sufficiently between freedom of thought and freedom of action. It may be a good thing for a man to keep an open mind about all his beliefs so that he will never claim for them absolute certainty and never dismiss entirely from his mind the thought that he may be wrong. But where there is a call for action, he must act on what he believes to be true. The lawyer, who in this respect stands midway between the philosopher and the man of action, does not allow himself to act on any sort of belief. He requires to be satisfied beyond reasonable doubt. If he is so satisfied he would then think it right to punish a man for a breach of the law while acknowledging the possibility that he may be mistaken. Is there any difference, so far as the freedom of the individual is concerned, between punishing a man for an act which admittedly he did and which we believe, but perhaps erroneously, to be wrong, he denying that it is wrong; and punishing him for an act that is admittedly wrong and which we honestly, but perhaps erroneously, believe that he did, he denying that he did it?

Philosophers may philosophize under the shadow of perpetual doubt but the governors of society cannot do their duty if they are not permitted to act upon what they believe. Here we may perhaps usefully return to what Mill said about Marcus Aurelius. He cited him as an example of the fallibility of even the best and wisest of men. Marcus Aurelius thought Christianity wholly unbelievable and could see in it only a force that would cause the society he governed to fall into pieces. Mill did not regard Christianity as an unmixed blessing, but it might have been a different thing, he thought, if adopted under Marcus Aurelius instead of under Constantine. So, Mill urged, unless a man flatters himself that he is wiser and better than Marcus Aurelius, let him abstain from that assumption of joint infallibility of himself and the multitude which the great man made with such unfortunate results.

The example is a fair one on the point of fallibility. If we were to be confronted with a creed which taught that constraint was the only vice and the unlimited indulgence of the appetites of all sorts the only virtue worth cultivating, we should look at it without any comprehension at all. But I dare say that our contempt would not be greater than that of Marcus Aurelius for Christianity or that of a medieval philosopher for the notion that heresy should be tolerated.

But the example is a fair one also on the point that I am making.

What else, one may ask, did Mill expect Marcus Aurelius to do? It is idle to lament that he did not forestall Constantine in accepting Christianity, for he could not accept what he disbelieved. In Mill's view and probably in that of most of his disciples Marcus Aurelius was right in rejecting the claims of Christianity. On this view the Emperor's mistake lay in his failure to realize that, if he permitted the destruction of his society through the agency of a religion which he rightly concluded to be false, the succeeding civilization would be an improvement upon his.

To put Mill's question again but in this other context, can any man putting himself in the position of the great emperor flatter himself that he would have acted more wisely? It is not feasible to require of any society that it should permit its own destruction by that which, whether rightly or wrongly, it honestly believes to be error, in case it may be mistaken. To admit that we are not infallible is not to admit that we are always wrong. What we believe to be evil may indeed be evil and we cannot for ever condemn ourselves to inactivity against evil because of the chance that we may by mistake destroy good. For better or worse the law-maker must act according to his lights and he cannot therefore accept Mill's doctrine as practicable even if as an ideal he thought it to be desirable.

But I must say for my part that I do not accept it as an ideal. I accept it as an inspiration. What Mill taught about the value of freedom of inquiry and the dangers of intolerance has placed all free men for ever in his debt. His admonitions were addressed to a society that was secure and strong and hidebound. Their repetition today is to a society much less solid. As a tract for the times, what Mill wrote was superb, but as dogma it has lost much of its appeal. For Mill's doctrine is just as dogmatic as any of those he repudiates. It is dogmatic to say that if only we were all allowed to behave just as we liked so long as we did not injure each other, the world would become a better place for all of us. There is no more evidence for this sort of Utopia than there is for the existence of Heaven and there is nothing to show that the one is any more easily attained than the other. We must not be bemused by words. If we are not entitled to call our society 'free' unless we pursue freedom to an extremity that would make society intolerable for most of us, then let us stop short of the extreme and be content with some other name. The result may not be freedom unalloyed, but there are alloys which strengthen without corrupting.

VII

Morals and Contemporary Social Reality*

Those who have followed the current controversy about the relationship between law and morals have now a number of doctrines to choose from. First and foremost, there is Mill's doctrine of liberty enunciated in 1859. Then there is the doctrine of Mr. Justice Stephen contained in his work *Liberty, Equality, Fraternity*, published in 1873, in which interest has recently been revived because of Professor Hart's detailed study of it in his book *Law, Liberty and Morality*. Then there is the statement of principle in the Wolfenden Committee's Report that 'there must remain a realm of private morality and immorality which is, in brief and crude terms, not the law's business'.[1] Then there is the first lecture in this book. Mr. Justice Stephen and myself can hardly claim doctrinal status; but we have been noticed because, as Professor Hart puts it, 'though their arguments are at points confused, they certainly still deserve the compliment of rational opposition'.[2] Then there are other modern statements of principle, notably by Dr. St. John-Stevas.

It is not therefore premature to inquire what is the doctrine held by Professor Hart.

There are at present four things to be said about that. The first is that it is not the doctrine enunciated by Mill, though Professor Hart still gives pride of place to 'the famous sentence'[3] which is the core of Mill on liberty. Secondly, it has not yet been stated with that power of clarity and definition which Mill used so persuasively and which, I can say without flattery, Professor Hart is generally recognized also to possess. Thirdly, its nature has

---

* An address given to a reading party on law and morals at Cumberland Lodge, Windsor, on 20 April 1964.
[1] Wolfenden, para. 61.   [2] Hart, p. 17.
[3] ibid. p. 4. The famous sentence is quoted at p. 103 *supra*.

so far been revealed only accidentally in the course of Professor Hart's attempts to bring Mill's doctrine into contact with 'contemporary social reality'. Fourthly, it will, when it is stated, probably be well grounded on *terra firma* because it is one of Professor Hart's general objections to the views of Stephen and myself that they are not. 'Stephen's doctrine, and much of Lord Devlin's,' Professor Hart writes, 'may seem to hover in the air above the *terra firma* of contemporary social reality; it may be a well-articulated construction, interesting because it reveals the outlook of the English judiciary but lacking application to contemporary society.'[1]

I do not know that this is the outlook of the English judiciary. Certainly they are more often accused by their academic critics of crawling about on *terra firma* with their noses on the ground than of hovering above it. But in this case, and pursuing as I was an extra-judicial activity, I must at once admit the charge. I did not think that the argument had anything to do with contemporary social reality. I thought that it was completely doctrinaire. After all, Mill's doctrine has existed for over a century and no one has ever attempted to put it into practice. The vast majority of people in this country still believe that certain practices are morally wrong and are content that they should be forbidden by the law as such. There are groups of active and intelligent people who propose legal reforms which are thought to involve some impairment of moral principle, for example, about abortion and euthanasia. But no one goes so far as to suggest that abortions and killings of consenting adults are not part of the law's business. The recommendation of the Wolfenden Committee that homosexuality between consenting adults should no longer be criminal, in spite of the fact that it was backed by the overwhelming majority of its members, has not gained popular approval. On a free vote in the House of Commons in 1960 it was turned down by a large majority. If ever a bill of reform is introduced to give effect to it, it will, I venture to think, be supported only on the practical grounds which are so powerfully set out in the Report; and any ardent theorist who tries to tell the assembled legislators that their duty is without further ado to repeal a law that it was never their business to enact, is likely to be pulled down by the coat-tails by the contemporary realists behind him.

The pressure of opinion that in the end makes and unmakes laws is not to be found in the mouths of those who talk most about

[1] Hart, p. 63.

morality and reform, but in the hearts of those who continue without much reflection to believe most of what they learnt from their fathers and to teach their children likewise. What they believe may be quite wrong: but it is quite contemporary and quite real. So in a democracy the existing laws contain the best and most comprehensive statement of contemporary social reality. They are not a perfect statement. There is always some unrepealed junk that nobody will make the effort to get rid of. Moreover, of its nature the law cannot be immediately responsive to new developments and may need as a corrective the observation of the man up aloft who gauges the strength and direction of the winds of change. It is, for example, an arguable statement that the exaction of the death penalty is an antiquated idea on its way out. I dare say that the majority still favours its retention but probably with a declining belief in its value; and the House of Commons has actually voted in favour of its abolition. But at least until the point is reached when there is strong pressure against a particular law, the ideas of reformers, however well and articulately expressed, are not contemporary social reality but wishful thinking about the sort of society they would like to see; and if and when they become contemporary, it is improbable that they will take the exact form of the wishful thoughts. At present there is no real pressure whatever—the sort of pressure that governments have to take account of sooner or later—for any reform of the law based on the extrusion of moral principle. Mill's doctrine of liberty has made no conquests on *terra firma*.

I have not said any of this so as to decry the value of advanced thinking. I protest only against the notion that everyone who does not assent to the immediate colonization of all the territory that has been reconnoitred and skirmished over is lacking in a sense of contemporary reality. Nor did I use the word 'doctrinaire' contemptuously. I believe that arguments about doctrine are useful as well as interesting. I do not suppose that a doctrine, such as Mill's on liberty, will ever be adopted or that law will ever be made in accordance with the principles he laid down. Examination over the years has revealed too many impracticabilities and possibly also, as Professor Hart suggests, 'theoretical deficiencies'.[1] But there is in it a vein of truth that has influenced immensely those who have studied it and will continue to do so. Undoubtedly, Professor Hart would agree with that, though he and I would differ profoundly about what is truth

[1] Hart, p. 16.

and what is error. That is a battle worth fighting but it has nothing whatever to do with contemporary social reality.

For these reasons I doubt whether it is now profitable to consider Mill's doctrine, except perhaps incidentally, in terms of its applicability to social reality. Certainly, it is not for the opponents of the doctrine, such as Mr. Justice Stephen and myself in matters of morals, to determine how it is to be applied. The most that we can do—and perhaps as much as it is legitimate to do—is to draw the attention of Mill's disciples to the fact that there is in England, as in all countries there always has been, a great deal of law that is inconsistent with the doctrine and to inquire what, if anything, they propose should be done about it. In fact, both Stephen and I made this inquiry, introducing it with what Professor Hart has called some 'not very perspicuous remarks'.[1]

Mill left the answer to Stephen's inquiry to his disciple, John Morley, who dismissed as 'bustling ponderosity' this appeal to contemporary social reality. It was, he said, wholly irrelevant. The question was not what the laws were but what they ought to be. The controversy has, I think, remained at this high theoretical level until Professor Hart brought a practical mind to bear on it. Incidentally, Morley had opportunities rarely obtained by a rationalist philosopher of putting his theories into practice. He was a Member of Parliament for a great many years and one of the four men who formed the dominant group in Mr. Gladstone's last Cabinet. But he does not appear to have made any use of them.

Professor Hart does not take the high line. He acknowledges 'the innocuous conservative principle that there is a presumption that common and long established institutions are likely to have merits not apparent to the rationalist philosopher'.[2] I do not want here to assess the weight that should be given to the conservative principle. I think, if I may say so, that Professor Hart is right in thinking that with many minds its persuasive force would be very considerable; and that it is, so to speak, well worth his while to tackle the point and to clear up, if he can, what he says is the 'confused and confusing'[3] use made by Stephen and others, including myself, of examples taken from the existing law. These include two fundamental principles and eight specific crimes which prima facie are inconsistent with the doctrine that the criminal law should be used only to protect others from harm to which they do not consent. Professor

---

[1] Hart, p. 29.   [2] ibid. p. 29.   [3] ibid.

Hart would retain the two principles as clarified by himself, and two out of the eight specific crimes, namely, bigamy and cruelty to animals. One of the crimes, homosexuality, he would abolish. (I am of course considering these crimes only in so far as they relate to acts done in private between consenting adults.) There are five other crimes, namely, abortion, buggery in the form of bestiality, incest, obscenity, e.g. the sale of pornography, and offences connected with prostitution, such as pimping, poncing, and brothel keeping which can conveniently be categorized as the commercialization of vice. Professor Hart is silent about all of these, although there are indications that he would grant neither to abortion nor to the commercialization of vice the full protection afforded by the private realm.[1] Undoubtedly, protection was denied to the latter by the recommendations of the Wolfenden Committee on prostitution.

It would, I hope, not be too uncharitable to suppose that Professor Hart has selected those examples which he finds it most convenient to deal with; but it would also be churlish not to acknowledge that he is, I believe, the first high authority to condescend so far. It is a curious thing that a century after the statement of the doctrine it is still not possible to say what amendments to the criminal law would flow from it; and that there is only one crime, that of homosexuality, that is known with certainty to lie within the private realm.

I should like to review Professor Hart's treatment of these matters. My purpose is not to see how far Professor Hart has succeeded in his object, though inevitably my opinion will emerge that within the framework of Mill's statement of his doctrine he has failed. My purpose is to see what happens to Mill's doctrine in the process. It seems to me that it is bumped so severely on *terra firma* as to be battered out of all recognition; and that what Professor Hart is prepared to put in its place can be glimpsed only through a glass darkly.

The first clash of principle arises over the part played by morality in the assessment of punishment. Mill would not allow morality to play any part in the making of the law. The bulk of the criminal law is taken up with offences which have the two characteristics of being offences against the moral law and of causing physical harm to the persons or property of other individuals. It is the second characteristic only which in the eyes of Mill and his disciples justifies the existence of the law. But if what justifies the making of the law is

[1] See his remarks on reform in his preface.

simply the prevention of harm, the offender must be punished accordingly. He must be punished for theft as he would be, for example, for a parking offence; the penalty must be calculated to prevent the repetition of the offence by him and to deter others from committing it. The offender's moral guilt is not a matter with which the law is concerned.[1]

This is not how in fact the law is administered. The degree of moral guilt is not the only determinant of the severity of the sentence but it is universally regarded as a very important one. It manifests itself in two ways. Firstly, in the gradation of offences in the criminal calendar: in order of gravity they are not arranged simply according to the harm done. Secondly, by taking into account the wickedness in the way the crime is committed: sentences for theft are not graded simply according to the amount of money stolen nor even according to more refined methods of estimating the harm done.

Professor Hart does not, as one might think he would, advocate the extrusion of morality from the assessment of punishment. Instead, he distinguishes between the system of punishment, where-under only harmful conduct should be punished, and the quantum of punishment. He describes Stephen's failure to perceive the distinction between system and quantum as 'an illuminating error'.[2] I have a strong predisposition to think that there must be something in anything that is said by Professor Hart; but here I must admit failing to perceive either the error or what it illuminates. It is a doctrine firmly embedded in English law that power which is given for one purpose, whether to a minister or to a judge, must not be used for another purpose. That is abuse of power: and its prevention is essential to the existence of a free society. Under the law as it is now administered it would be an abuse of power to punish for immorality that is outside the law. It sometimes happens that an act which is a breach of the criminal law is also a breach of that part of the moral law that is not included in the criminal. Thus a course of deception might include an adultery. In such a case it would be wrong for the judge to increase the sentence appropriate to the crime because of the adultery. A judge may proportion his sentence according to the degree of immorality involved in the act itself but

---

[1] This is the view adopted by Lady Wootton in *Crime and the Criminal Law*, pp. 41 et seq. It would involve an upheaval of the criminal law which evidently does not commend itself to Professor Hart. [2] Hart, p. 34.

not according to extraneous immorality. On Mill's doctrine all immorality is extraneous. The moral content, if any, of an enactment is accidental and its presence or absence should make no difference.

Let me illustrate this by a comparison of morality with religion. The enactment of a law designed simply to enforce a religious belief would rightly be regarded as objectionable. Does this mean that we should now repeal a law which prohibits Sunday trading? Not necessarily, because it is desirable that there should be a universal day of rest and it might as well be Sunday as any other day; it can be justified on that ground. But would it then be proper, in the case of a breach by a practising Jew, to double the sentence on the ground that he was offending against a religious principle as well as against a social regulation? That would at once be condemned as bringing religion into the law. Why then is it permissible in the area of punishment to bring morality into the law?

Stephen's error, according to Professor Hart, lies in his 'failure to see that the questions "What sort of conduct may justifiably be punished?" and "How severely should we punish different offences?" are distinct and independent questions'.[1] I do not think that they are independent questions. They are a division, made for the sake of convenience, of the single question which is: 'What justifies the sentence of punishment?' The justification must be found in the law and there cannot be a law which is not concerned with a man's morals and yet which permits him to be punished for his immorality. If one can imagine a judge dividing a sentence into parts and sentencing a man to three months for the harm he has done to his victim and six months for his wickedness in doing it, the result would be just the same as if he had been separately charged under two separate sections of a statute, one which made the act an offence if done without any intent and another which made it a graver offence if done with a wicked intent. Consider a more plausible example of the sort given by Stephen. A judge says to the prisoner: 'This is your first offence and a petty theft. In ordinary circumstances I would have given you another chance. But this particular theft was a despicable one, the stealing of money from someone who had trusted and befriended you. I cannot overlook that and shall sentence you to three months imprisonment.' That is punishment for moral depravity and for nothing else.

[1] Hart, p. 36.

I do not quarrel with the reasons which Professor Hart gives for allowing moral considerations to enter into the assessment of punishment. He points out[1] that if the scale of punishments for crimes conflicted with common estimates of their comparative wickedness, moral judgements might be confused and the law brought into disrepute. Principles of justice or fairness between different offenders, he says, require morally distinguishable offences to be treated differently and morally similar offences to be treated alike. I agree with this. But it seems to me to force his withdrawal from the firm line that the law is not concerned with morality as such. He says: '. . . in the theory of punishment, what is in the end morally tolerable is apt to be more complex than our theories initially suggest. We cannot usually in social life pursue a single value or a single moral aim, untroubled by the need to compromise with others.'[2] This, if I may say so, is excellent sense. But why only 'in the theory of punishment'? These are considerations which apply with equal force to the making of the law—to the question whether there should, for example, be a law against homosexuality at all. If the statutes in question were to be repealed, moral judgements might be confused and the law brought into disrepute because people would see moral wickedness going unpunished. That is one of the arguments against repeal. Against that there are the arguments of the misery caused to individuals and so on. The answer may be a compromise. But Professor Hart will not compromise on this because he says homosexuality is within the realm into which the law has no claim to enter; he cannot therefore discuss terms of entry. This is a theoretical proposition and must be defended as such.

Neither can there be any compromise in the theory of punishment. If by any chance Mill's doctrine had become the law and what we were discussing was how to make an impracticable piece of theory work in a way which would give as little dissatisfaction as possible to sensible people, then what Professor Hart says would be very much in point. But what we are discussing is quite different. It is whether the theory that the law may not be used to enforce morality as such is consistent with the theory that punishment under law may be adjusted according to the moral gravity of the act done. To my mind it clearly is not; and it seems to me to be an emasculation of Mill's doctrine to say that it is to apply only to the making of the law and not to the administration of it.

[1] Hart, pp. 36–7.　　　　　　　[2] ibid. p. 38.

The second fundamental principle has to do with the function of consent in the criminal law. Mill's doctrine should make it always a good defence because the law should be concerned only with harming another against his will. But in general, consent is no defence, though there are crimes, such as rape and larceny, in which the absence of consent is an ingredient of the offence and has to be proved by the prosecution accordingly. One example of the ordinary crimes to which consent is no defence is murder in cases of euthanasia, duelling, and suicide pacts. Another is assault; some form of masochism would perhaps today be the most likely case of a willing submission to an assault.

The conclusion which I drew from this in my first lecture was that a breach of the criminal law was regarded as an offence not merely against the person injured but against society as a whole; and that an act done by consent, such as euthanasia, could be prohibited only as the breach of a moral principle which society required to be observed. Professor Hart says roundly that this 'is simply not true'.[1] The emphasis suggests that I have overlooked the obvious. What, alas, I did not foresee was that some of the crew who sail under Mill's flag of liberty would mutiny and run paternalism up the mast. Professor Hart considers that it is paternalism and not moral principle that is the justification of the law in these matters and he is thereby enabled to accept the second principle. 'The rules excluding the victim's consent as a defence to charges of murder or assault may perfectly well be explained as a piece of paternalism, designed to protect individuals against themselves.'[2]

'Mill no doubt might have protested', Professor Hart goes on in a meiosis which deserves to be commemorated. This tears the heart out of his doctrine. 'His own good either physical or moral is not a sufficient warrant. He cannot rightfully be compelled to do or forbear because it will be better for him to do so, because it will make him happier, because in the opinions of others, to do so would be wise or even right'.[3]

Professor Hart suggests that Mill might have objected not quite as much to paternalism as to the enforcement of moral principle.[4] He bases this on Mill's particularization of the three grounds on which compulsion would be wrongful. These, he says, are separate, the first two as I understand it, referring to paternalism, and the third

---

[1] Hart, p. 31.   [2] ibid.   [3] Mill, *On Liberty*, p. 72.
[4] I suggest *infra* at p. 136 that there is no real distinction between the two.

to enforcement of morality. This seems to me a forced reading. Mill states his reasons cumulatively and not alternatively. If a man does what is wise and right, surely in Mill's view it would make him better and happier; he would not have distinguished between them. But anyway Professor Hart makes it quite plain that if the doctrine is divisible he abandons at least half of it.

I think, if I may say so without impertinence, that Professor Hart's argument might have been clearer if he had left Mill out of it. He gains no advantage by citing Mill as an authority. If Mill was obviously wrong about paternalism, why should he be right about enforcement of morals? Freed from the incubus of Mill, Professor Hart would doubtless have stated in his own words and with his customary precision how he defined the boundaries of the private realm. As it is, he does it by means of what he describes without overstatement as a 'modification'[1] of Mill. I for one am left in genuine doubt about what the modification is.

Clearly it must be one that will accommodate paternalism at least to some extent. But will that be complete paternalism, i.e., in respect of all that makes a man better and happier? Or is a distinction being drawn between a man's physical good and his moral good? Is Professor Hart, so to speak, a physical paternalist and a moral individualist? I believe that one would have the answer to this if only one knew exactly what the distinction was between paternalism and legal moralism. The neglect of this distinction is, Professor Hart says, 'a form of a more general error'.[2] But what is legal moralism? It occurs when judges go 'out of their way to express the view that the enforcement of sexual morality is a proper part of the law's business'.[3] That is all that Professor Hart says about it.

But what exactly is it? If it is only a reprehensible judicial habit of moralizing *obiter*, it cannot be contrasted with paternalism so as to produce an illuminating distinction. Is it perhaps only another way of describing paternalism in matters of morality, which I shall call for short moral paternalism? This makes the whole argument readily comprehensible, provided only that it is possible to draw a line (which, for reasons I shall give, I think that it is not) between physical and moral paternalism.

If that is not the distinction, then it must lie between legal moralism and complete paternalism, that is, presumably, between the use of the law to enforce morals and its use to force a man to do what

[1] Hart, p. 33.   [2] ibid. p. 34.   [3] ibid. p. 6.

is for his own moral good. This is undoubtedly the distinction that fits in best with the language used by Professor Hart; he never expressly qualifies the use of the paternalism he advocates and there are passages in the text that suggest it to be of the widest kind. But then would not complete paternalism justify laws against immorality? (When talking of immorality in this part of the argument I had better restrict it to homosexuality because that is, as I have said, the only immorality which we know for certain is in Professor Hart's view both covered by the existing criminal law and included within the private realm as not the law's business.) Surely paternalism would make homosexuality the law's business if it is morally harmful to the man who is being paternalized. Yet if there is one thing that is clear, it is that Professor Hart wholeheartedly supports the Wolfenden Committee's recommendation that the law against homosexuality should be repealed on the ground that it is not the law's business.

Let me consider how 'the famous sentence' in Mill would have to be restated so as to cover these alternative hypotheses.

Firstly, on the assumption that it has to cover only physical paternalism. Then it could read as follows. 'The only purposes for which power can rightfully be exercised over any member of a civilized community against his will are to prevent harm to others or for his own physical good. His own moral good is not a sufficient warrant. He can rightfully be compelled to do or forbear because it will be physically better for him to do so or because it will make him [?physically] happier, but not because in the opinions of others, to do so would be wise or even right.'

Secondly, on the assumption that it has to cover complete paternalism, physical and moral. Then it would have to read as follows. 'The only purposes for which power can rightfully be exercised over any member of a civilized community against his will are to prevent harm to others or for his own physical or moral good. His own good either physical or moral is therefore a sufficient warrant. He can rightfully be compelled to do or forbear because it will be better for him to do so or because it will make him happier, but not because in the opinions of others, to do so would be wise or even right.'

Clearly, the first restatement is less unattractive than the second. Its apologists who are prepared to believe that the doctrine is divisible can claim for this version that the amendment does not annihilate much more than half the doctrine and so might be described as an act of modification. The second restatement, I think it would have to be admitted, injures the whole doctrine almost to the point of destruction by direct contradiction and adds to the injury the insult of reducing it to nonsense. If the law will not let a man judge for himself whether an act will make him better and happier, how can it be judged except by the opinions of others? And if in the opinions of others the act is unwise or wrong, how could it in their opinion make him better and happier?

I shall now examine the distinction between physical and moral paternalism on which the first restatement is based. When dealing with the exclusion of consent as a defence to murder or assault, Professor Hart uses a phrase which suggests that he might be drawing a distinction between physical and moral paternalism. He refers to 'using the law to protect even a consenting victim from *bodily* harm'.[1] But I do not think that—at least in this connexion—he can mean the word 'bodily' to be distinctive. It would be quite unrealistic to treat the crimes with which Professor Hart is dealing as offences against the body of the consenting party and not against morals. The most common case of a man willingly submitting to assault would, as I have suggested, be a case of masochism. To say that the law should intervene there not because of the vice but to protect the man in his own best interests from getting bodily hurt hardly seems sense. So in euthanasia. It cannot seriously be suggested that, if there were no moral principle involved, the law in a free country would tell a man when he was and when he was not to die, obtaining its mandate from its paternal interest in his body and not in his soul. Or that in euthanasia the crime lies not in the moral decision to seek death but purely in the physical and no doubt painless act that causes it.

If however there is an element of physical paternalism in the law that forbids masochism and euthanasia these crimes seem to me as good examples as any that could be selected to illustrate the difficulty in practice of distinguishing between physical and moral paternalism. Neither in principle nor in practice can a line be drawn between legislation controlling the individual's physical welfare and legislation controlling his moral welfare. If paternalism be the principle, no father of a family would content himself with looking after his children's welfare and leaving their morals to themselves. If society has an interest which permits it to legislate in the one case, why not

[1] Hart, p. 31. The italics are mine.

in the other? If, on the other hand, we are grown up enough to look after our own morals, why not after our own bodies?

The terms in which Professor Hart justifies the sort of paternalism he advocates lead to the same conclusion. There is, he says, 'a general decline in the belief that individuals know their own interests best'.[1] There can be no reason to believe that if unable to perceive their own physical good unaided, they can judge of their own moral good. He continues: 'Choices may be made or consent given without adequate reflection or appreciation of the consequences; or in pursuit of merely transitory desires; or in various predicaments when the judgment is likely to be clouded; or under inner psychological compulsion; or under pressure by others of a kind too subtle to be susceptible of proof in a law court.'[2] These words, it seems to me, might almost have been written with homosexuals in mind. It is moral weakness rather than physical that leads to predicaments when the judgement is likely to be clouded and is the cause of inner psychological compulsion.

These considerations drive one to the conclusion that a distinction between moral and physical paternalism is not what Professor Hart has in mind. But the alternative hypothesis seems even more unacceptable. If it is difficult to draw a line between moral and physical paternalism, it is impossible to draw one of any significance between moral paternalism and the enforcement of the moral law. A moral law, that is, a public morality, is a necessity for paternalism, otherwise it would be impossible to arrive at a common judgement about what would be for a man's moral good. If then society compels a man to act for his own moral good, society is enforcing the moral law; and it is a distinction without a difference to say that society is acting for a man's own good and not for the enforcement of the law. Does the avoidance of legal moralism mean no more than that a judge ought not, when passing sentence, to mention that he is enforcing the law but only that he is acting for a man's own good?

Even this distinction vanishes if, as Professor Hart holds, a judge is entitled when passing sentence to take into account the breach of the moral law. In such circumstances a sentence that avoided legal moralism would have to be framed on the following lines. 'John Doe and Richard Roe, you have pleaded guilty to an act of gross indecency. In this country we regard such acts as morally wrong, but you are not standing in the dock because of that. You are in the

---

[1] Hart, p. 32.   [2] ibid. p. 33.

dock because you have broken a law that was passed for your own moral good and because it is my duty to prevent you from breaking it again. If I were considering only your own good, I should bind you over on condition that you submitted to psychiatric treatment. But the law says that in order not to confuse moral judgements or to bring the law itself into disrepute, I am when passing sentence to have regard to the moral wickedness of your act. I shall therefore sentence you each to three months' imprisonment.'

Finally, if it is possible, which I doubt, to draw a theoretical distinction between moral paternalism and the enforcement of morality, it is not one that is relevant to the present argument. The issue is whether there is a realm of private morality and immorality that is not the law's business. Paternalism, unless it is limited in some way as yet unstated, must, as I have pointed out, make all morality the law's business.

So both the restatements I have been considering lead to untenable, if not absurd, positions. Whatever modification Professor Hart contemplates is hardly likely to lead to absurdity. He must have in mind some substitution which he has yet to formulate.

In addition to the necessity for accommodating paternalism, a restatement or new statement will have to allow for other modifications which Professor Hart is prepared to admit. The offence of cruelty to animals can be accommodated if protection from harm is extended beyond humanity to all sentient beings. Some such thought may well have been in Mill's mind; for in his definition of the standard of morality in his *Utilitarianism* he refers not only to 'all mankind' but also 'so far as the nature of things admits, to the whole sentient creation'.[1] Yet he did not go beyond mankind in 'the famous sentence'. It is not at once apparent how the modification would fit in with it, for if (apart from an obligation to refrain from cruelty as morally harmful to the perpetrator) a duty towards animals is admitted, it is not of the same kind as a duty towards other members of the same society.

Bigamy is also a crime which Professor Hart is prepared to accept on the ground that it is a public act offensive to religious feelings.[2] He thinks it doubtful whether Mill would have allowed the punishment of bigamy on this ground. Mill's own exception in respect of public acts was expressed as covering those which 'are a violation

---

[1] Mill, p. 11.   [2] Hart, p. 42.

of good manners' in which category he placed 'offences against decency'.[1]

Bigamy violates neither good manners nor decency. It is therefore a difficult crime for Mill's disciples to deal with. When it is committed without deception it harms no one; yet in these days of easy divorce bigamists do not arouse sympathy as homosexuals do and no one is very enthusiastic about altering the law in their favour. A variety of reasons for leaving the law as it is have been put forward, but the one selected by Professor Hart seems to me to wound Mill's doctrine more sharply than any other. A marriage in a registry office is only in form a public act. Mill's exception is grounded not upon a formal distinction between public and private but upon the right of society not to have obnoxious conduct forced on its attention. No one with deep religious feelings is likely to attend in the registry office; and the chance of the happy couple as they leave the office running into a man who happens to combine deep religious feelings with the knowledge that one of the parties has been married before is remote.

We have now reached a position in which the exceptions to Mill's doctrine must be expanded to cover the whole field of criminal punishment, some form of paternalism and offences against religious susceptibilities; and we are still left with five crimes about which Professor Hart says nothing. They are a diverse lot. It would be futile for me to try to anticipate the further series of modifications that would be necessary to accommodate them. I venture to think that Professor Hart's treatment of Mill has already proceeded far beyond the permissible limits of exegesis or even of amendment.

That completes the survey of the so-called modifications of Mill. It is not, I think, pedantic to insist that if they are to win any degree of acceptance, or even of understanding, they must be stated with a much higher degree of exactness. After all, Mill's doctrine of liberty, be it right or wrong, was formulated carefully and comprehensively and with exemplary clarity. It deserves the compliment of more precise treatment than it has received at the hands of Professor Hart. Until there has been a satisfactory restatement of it or a replacement of it by some other statement of comparable merit, there appears to me to be no room for any further discussion at the theoretical level.

At the practical level I think also with respect that Professor Hart's

---

[1] Mill, p. 153.

treatment of the subject is defective. At this level I assume that the purpose is to further the sort of reforms of the criminal law which Professor Hart mentions in the preface to his book. I do not doubt that a strong case can be made out for each of them taken by itself and on its own merits. There can be no practical reason for invoking some general principle of liberty in moral behaviour unless it is to cover a group of reforms which thus united in principle have an appeal which taken singly each would lack. If the statement that 'there must remain a realm of private morality and immorality, which is, in brief and crude terms, not the law's business' is meant only as a slogan to draw attention in a dramatic way to the fact that homosexual offences are usually committed in private and without direct injury except to the participants, it is not worth further comment whether at the practical or theoretical level. If it is really meant as a statement of principle to include other immoralities besides the homosexual, every practical reformer before he makes use of it will want to be told what else it embraces. To do as Professor Hart does and to pick out one or two offences which it excludes will win no adherents. What those interested in reform will want to know is whether, if the principle is conceded in the case of homosexuality, some other and what parts of the existing criminal law will be carried away as well. Incest? Abortion? Bestiality? Does the principle cover legislation against brothels and pornography; and if not, why not? These are not questions that can be shirked indefinitely by anyone who regards the principle as relevant to contemporary social reality.